The Gift of Infidelity

HEALING SELF-BETRAYAL AND C-PTSD

ANDREA MERKL

Copyright © 2024 by Andrea Merkl

All rights reserved. Without limiting the rights under copyright reserved above, no part of of this publication may be reproduced, stored in or introduced into a retrieval system, or transmitted in any form or by any means (electronic, mechanical, photocopying, recording or otherwise), without the prior written permission of both the copyright owner and the above publisher of this book.

ISBN: 978-1-7390629-0-3

Published in association with The Self Publishing Agency

For my daughters,
COLETTE AND SIMONE

I am like water.
Fluid and ever changing.
I take shape to my surroundings.
I curve around rocks, flow over debris,
and grow stronger with force.
I act as a reflection to others,
my light illuminates to guide the way.
I flow with the current,
letting love set the course.

Contents

THE REALIZATION 1

PART ONE

She Never Sees It Coming 3

D-day 3
What we want, wants us 8
Chaos and order 10

PART TWO

All His Fault. For Sure 15

Bathroom floor moment 15
Emotional rollercoaster 18
Unconscious marriage 20

PART THREE

My Brutiful Frenemy Self-Betrayal 31

It's not me, it's you 31
Healing trauma 39
Baptism by fire 43

PART FOUR

Doping Out on Facebook 51

Some holy shit 51
Instagram God 52
Being real women 60
Forgiveness like a thawing river 61

PART FIVE

My Triathlon Year and Other Clichés 65

Faith and endurance 65
While it was still dark 70

PART SIX

Selfish Selflessness or Vice Versa 81

One of a pair 81
Letting go of what's not me 82
Anyone but her 90
The edge of chaos 92
Baptism redux 95

PART SEVEN

Totally Worth It. I Think 99

Replaced 99
Generations deep 109

PART EIGHT

The Scientific Art of Healing 115

The original betrayal 115
Becoming a neuroscientist 122
Forgiveness like a flowing river 128
An ever after love 134
My prayer for you 140

ACKNOWLEDGEMENTS 141

CRITICAL SOURCES 143

RESOURCES MENTIONED 149

THE REALIZATION

It was 2019. I was in church one day when a guest pastor was speaking. He started sharing a story from the Bible about a woman that longed for union and connection. A woman who thought she wasn't good enough. Not pretty enough, not smart enough, not funny enough. All the not-enoughs. She longed for a sense of belonging. Her name was Leah.

Well, her name might as well been Andrea because, Holy shit! I thought, I am Leah! I feel unloved, worthless, and rejected. I was cast aside. I sat there bawling in my seat as I continued to listen, taking in each word like I wrote this story, like it was a mirror into my soul.

The pastor continued to explain that her soon-to-be husband Jacob wanted to marry her sister Rachel, who was praised as the more beautiful sister, but Leah's father felt she should be married first, being the oldest daughter. So, using Leah's veil to cover her face, he switched the sisters. You know, the old veil switcheroo. What was that veil made of anyway, lead? Maybe it was a midnight wedding. I am just going to give the Bible the benefit of the doubt for now.

Ok, so the pastor continued sharing that the wedding day and night came and the next morning Jacob awoke to Leah lying beside him. Dissatisfied and feeling tricked, he married her sister Rachel a week later. Leah was left feeling unloved, abandoned, and rejected. So now Jacob had two wives. Imagine their two tents side by side. Jacob is living his best life, Leah not so much. During this trial God blessed Leah with many children. Her second child was named Simeon, which meant, "He who has heard," or *God has heard*. God knew of Leah's heartache and was taking her on a journey. He longed for a relationship with her and wanted her to see that no matter how much a human being loved or did not love her, it could not compare to the everlasting love and security that he provided.

PART ONE

⠿

She Never Sees It Coming

D-DAY

My whole world collapsed around me as I sat on my childhood bed at my parents' house at 3:00 a.m. Eight months pregnant with our second child, and my swollen stomach contracting. I thought I might go into labour right there. My body rejecting the fact that this could happen. That it could happen to me.

As I looked at my phone, seeing months and months of daily visits to the same location, scrolling through the location history, time stood still. I watched myself from outside my body.

This can't really be happening. We are about to have a baby. And then I suddenly snapped out of this trance by feeling the stabbing pains in my stomach. My heart pounding outside of my chest. Unsure if it was Braxton-Hicks contractions or my body experiencing the pain it had just discovered.

I called my husband and started to yell, "I know, I know. Just tell me the truth. Just say it. Just say it."

And he started to cry into the phone, "I can't say it. I can't."

I continued to scream, "You need to drive here right now!" He agreed. How could this have happened to me? I thought, This is the type of thing that happens to other people. I was frozen in shock. At the same time a sense of relief came over me because I was finally validated by the truth. A truth I had known deep down for the last nine months when the affair had started.

Everything I had known fell away and I was left with everything I didn't know. I was left with a newborn on the way, and her older sister sleeping in the next room. I was left feeling rejected, unloved, and scared. And I was so confused. Who was my husband? This couldn't be the person I married. Were the past eight years all a lie? I was in so much disbelief. This couldn't be happening; this was my person. The person I went to with my problems. With my hurt and pain. But now this person was the source of hurt and pain. I could not process that reality. I was in denial and didn't want to move. I was caught in a mental loop of this isn't real, this is real. This has really happened. But he would never do that. He must have a split personality because that was not the person I knew. All of my insecurities were brought to the surface. I felt not good enough. Not pretty enough. Not funny enough. Not smart enough. Not enough in all ways possible.

My husband drove to my parents' house where I was staying for the weekend. He said the affair was over. I didn't know what I would do when I saw him. When he arrived I cried and hugged him. My maternal instinct kicked in and my love for him pushed up to the surface. I just wanted us to be together, our family all together. I wanted to make our marriage work. I wanted to fix what was broken. I was due in a few weeks and felt I needed him. My worth was so tightly tied to him. To being a wife. To being a mother. I was going to fight for this marriage and our family. I was not giving up.

We stayed the week with my parents at their house, which seemed to act like a buffer or waiting room for reality to sink in. It was a safe space. Our daughter completed her swimming lessons, and we were able to have some support with childcare so we could take time to start to unpack what had happened.

It came time to move out from the waiting room of my parents' house and we headed back home. Although he was physically there in our house with us in the following weeks, he was mentally in another place. He had drifted far away, and I wasn't sure if he would come back.

My perception of reality continued to shatter and I fell into a deep dark place. Nothing mattered to me anymore. I didn't want to be pregnant any longer. I couldn't sleep. I couldn't eat. Our life we had built together flashed before my eyes daily. Birthdays, Christmases, our wedding, the birth of our first daughter. Disappearing as fast as they appeared. Family photos on our walls, haunting me as I walked by each day. The days were moving by in slow motion. I just wanted out of this nightmare. My due date getting closer and closer, my hope for our marriage drifting further and further.

He began to tell me he still loved the other woman and missed her. I was coming at this situation with such hope, positive that we could get through it together and now I was faced with the fact that he might not actually WANT to stay together. That he also loved someone else. Umm, what? You LOVE her? I thought to myself.

Ok, side note. I was an amateur boxer for a few years. I have taken many hard hits. I have even knocked someone down on the canvas. (They did get back up.)

Before you get too excited, let me paint this picture accurately for you. The boxing gym was in the unfinished basement of an old church. Think mildew, concrete, and lights that flicker off and on hanging from a ceiling. A scene you normally see in a scary movie.

My dad was friends with one of the coaches so he took me there for training until I felt less intimidated. I was around sixteen years old and one of two females in the club. This meant once I learnt to skip, and had a few rounds on the heavy bag, I had to spar. And remember there was only one other girl in the club, so I had to spar with guys. It took me awhile to get past the possibility of getting hit in the face, or worse, a bloody nose or being KO'd. And every time I saw someone's head snap back when I hit them in the face, I would apologize. I started to think, am I too nice for this sport?

Pushing through the discomfort, I began to spar regularly, which meant getting hit in the face, a lot.

After a year of training, I started to learn how to fight competitively. During my first fight my trainer forgot to put my mouth guard in for one of the rounds. Luckily, I didn't get my teeth knocked out. My second fight no one showed up in my weight class, so I automatically won. That was easy. My third fight was at an army base, and I was accompanied into the ring by bagpipes.

And that about sums it up, folks!

After three bouts I decided, my short-lived, three-year boxing career would come to an end.

I was more of a lover than a fighter.

Ok, back to him telling me he loved another woman. Cue rage.

I can tell you that this blow hurt the most. Having your husband say he loves someone else is worse than a punch to the face. And I don't wish this experience on anyone.

I just wanted control. I wanted to control the outcome. I wanted my husband back. I wanted things to be back to normal. I wanted to fight. Except this time, I wasn't in the ring. But I was going to do whatever it took.

I started to look for any and all information regarding affair recovery and came across a YouTube channel. Perfect! I thought. This will surely help me win.

In the infidelity and affair recovery circles, they talk about discovery day, known as D-day. There is life before D-day and life after D-day. There is no going back to normal. Life as I knew it was over. I didn't know what was lying ahead. Would this grenade be lethal? Would our marriage survive? We were just about to become a family of four, and suddenly that wasn't a sure thing. I just hadn't seen this coming.

My D-day came June 5, 2018. I started to wonder, when was the real D-day? If my D-day changed the course of history, then I wanted to know more about the original D-day.

You know the epic invasion of 1944 that changed the course of WWII.

I learned that I had the same date that Eisenhower had originally selected: June 5, 1944. However, bad weather on the days leading up to the operation caused it to be delayed for twenty-four hours, so they didn't invade until June 6th. Eisenhower told the troops: *"You are about to embark upon the Great Crusade, toward which we have striven these many months. The eyes of the world are upon you."* [1]

Well, this will for sure be the biggest crusade I will be on, I thought, so buckle up.

Yeah, I got this. I am a trained fighter, remember?

The thing is, I wasn't ready for battle at all. I had a newborn instead of armor strapped to my chest and I am pretty sure you can't take a baby into battle.

SO maybe all of this fight, fight, fight mentality I was receiving and trying to implement at the time from the affair recovery videos wasn't going to work. I needed to enlist other forces for help.

WHAT WE WANT, WANTS US

I went to therapy twice a week to get through the tangled web of emotions I was feeling and navigate the dark place I was in. My therapist would help me come back to the present moment and regulate my nervous system. I was starting to learn how to feel and release the strong emotions like rage, anxiety, depressive and intrusive thoughts.

We had been working together for the previous year, so I was so fortunate to have her ready to help me in this crisis. We had some good groundwork laid out from the months prior. We had been doing hypnotherapy and I was able to access this space of calm and homeostasis at the appointment. Even if it was for just an hour, I could find some reprieve.

She reminded me one day of a time not too long previously when my husband and I were trying to become pregnant with this baby that was about to be born. We had a hard time becoming pregnant the second time. It took a couple years. And those years took a toll on my mental health, which was left unchecked. The anxiety and depression would accumulate each month when I saw a negative result on a pregnancy test. It became all-consuming. She said something to me that brought tears to my eyes, and I still remember to this day. "What if your baby is trying to get to you as much as you are trying to get to her/him?" We would do hypnotherapy and relaxation sessions, which started to calm down my nervous system. One day while doing one of the hypnotherapy sessions at home on my own, I was in deep relaxation, envisioning my womb space in a bright orange colour, like many times before over the previous months, but this time I saw a baby in the orange sphere. The next month I became pregnant.

This memory reminded me of a Rumi quote: "When I run after what I think I want, my days are a furnace of stress and anxiety. If I sit in my own place of patience, what I need flows to me and without any pain. *From this I understand that what I want also wants me, is looking for me and attracting me.* There is a great secret in this for everyone that can grasp it."

CHAOS AND ORDER

Still in the house together with my husband and trying to repair our relationship, I was living in a parallel existence between love and hate. I loved him and at the same time, I hated him. I had built a life with this person for the past eight years and in my mind there was only one option: staying together, no matter the cost.

As my doula and I had our last appointment and talked about what this birth could look like, she asked if I wanted my husband to be there. A question I never thought I would hear in my life. Ugh, that was a hard one. On one hand, of course I did. This was one of the most monumental moments a parent experiences in their life, and I still loved him. On the other hand, my heart was an open wound and he was the one that caused this injury.

I knew I would regret it if I didn't allow him to be there, so I decided it would be best for him and for me and for the baby if he were there.

My doula and I were trying everything under the sun to prepare me mentally and physically for the upcoming birth. We both thought that with the situation with my husband being so in flux, and my nervous system being in fight, flight, or freeze mode, there was no way that labor would ensue naturally. It would take a miracle. My body might have been chased by a tiger for all it knew, but it understood just what to do. And it would do it in its perfect and divine timing, two weeks early in fact. It's funny, life doesn't automatically stop when challenges arrive. Literally, life did not stop. Instead, new life was born in chaos.

June 5, 2018, my life was forever changed. And a few weeks later on July 5th, our second daughter would come into the world. In the midst of chaos, a baby was born.

I was so happy for our daughter to finally be here. All of my fears fell away when I looked at her. As the nurse laid her beside me on the bed, I just kept saying, "I am so happy she is finally here." Pressing my cheek against hers. Soaking up her newborn smell. Like I had known her a lifetime already.

Our little girl brought so much joy in such a dark time. She was a beacon of light. A lighthouse in a storm. Born at the perfect time.

I had time to read many books, having just giving birth, and nursing a lot. One of the books was *A New Earth: Awakening to Your Life's Purpose* by Eckhart Tolle.

He includes an interesting story in the book about a Zen master that lived in the late seventeenth and early eighteenth centuries. His name was Zen Master Hakuin. He is said to have created the now-famous question: "What is the sound of one hand clapping?" Hakuin believed that the understanding arising out of practice in everyday life was deeper than the understanding that could come from practicing in the monastery, since lay people faced more distractions, held more responsibilities, and experienced more heartbreak than the monks and so needed to practice with greater diligence.

Hakuin was greatly respected and had many disciples. At one time in his life, he lived in a village hermitage, close to a food shop run by a couple and their beautiful, young daughter. One day the parents discovered that their daughter was pregnant. Angry and distraught, they demanded to know the name of the father. At first, the girl would not confess but after much harassment, she named Hakuin. The furious parents confronted Hakuin, berating him in front of all of his students. He simply replied, "Is that so?"

When the baby was born, the family gave it to Hakuin. By this time, he had lost his reputation and his disciples. But Hakuin was not disturbed. He took delight in caring for the infant child; he was able to obtain milk and other essentials from the villagers. A year later, the young mother of the child was troubled by great remorse. She confessed the truth to her parents—the real father was not Hakuin but rather a young man who worked at the local fish market. The mortified parents went to Hakuin, apologizing, asking his forgiveness for the wrong they did him. They asked Hakuin to return the baby. Although he loved the child as his own, Hakuin was willing to give him up without complaint. All he said was: "Is that so?"

My daughter asleep beside me, all swaddled up. She was so beautiful and perfect. And this situation was far from perfect.

I looked at her after reading this and thought, How can anything be "Is this so?" I was so far away from the acceptance of the way things were. I couldn't relate to the story of Hakuin at all.

This wasn't what I wanted. This wasn't what I wanted for her or her sister. This wasn't the way I wanted my life to turn out. This wasn't supposed to happen to me.

I wanted things to be my way. The "right" way, our family being all together. The spiral back down into darkness returned. The newborn high of postpartum motherhood started to wear off and the pain started to take over again. The realization started to occur that this wasn't all nightmare but in fact very real.

PART TWO

All His Fault. For Sure

BATHROOM FLOOR MOMENT

It had been a month or so since I had given birth. On my knees on the bathroom floor, my T-shirt drenched in tears, I was inconsolable. "God help me," I cried. "Please help me." I was in deep despair. The darkest moment of my life came right after one of the lightest—the birth of my daughter. What a juxtaposition.

I wanted the pain to go away. I wanted my husband back. I wanted my family all together. I had just given birth, but this pain was so much worse. I thought my life was over. But it couldn't be over. I had two small humans to take care of. I had to get up off the bathroom floor and feed my newborn. I had to wake up every morning and take my preschooler to school. I had to be present for them, attend to their needs, and provide love for them. Love that I didn't know if I had in me anymore.

Real faith comes out of real need. I was in real need. Extreme need. I was thrown into a situation where I needed God so badly, I couldn't even think of surviving in my own strength.

I was in unfamiliar territory. Unable to self-soothe, regulate my emotions, or process what had happened. Out of desperation, I started praying prayers of forgiveness, of letting go, of empathy, and of gratitude.

I always thought of God as something that was far away, an external source. A few months after the initial disclosure of the affair, I had a spiritual awakening reading Marianne Williamson's book, *A Return to Love*. I had a realization that God is love, and we are all, in our purest essence, love. God lives inside of us. This can be referred to as the Holy Spirit, the Divine, Source, or Infinite Intelligence. Everyone experiences this presence in their own way.

I think this was the moment that I truly felt the presence of the Holy Spirit. Compassion started to flow through me. Forgiveness started to flood my body and heart. The strength that was given to me was something I could not have produced on my own. Grace upon grace continued to flow over me.

When I started to turn inward and discover this unconditional love that existed inside of me, things started to change. The more I developed self-love, then the more I felt this intimacy with God. The more I developed this intimacy with God, the more I felt this self-love. They were interchangeable.

---

1 John 4:16   *God is love. Whoever lives in love lives in God, and God in them.*

I also found the Prayer of Saint Francis in one of the books I was reading and I read it daily in an effort to find some solace, peace, and comfort. Funny enough, throughout all my Catholic upbringing I had never heard this prayer. Still, I have had a belief in God since I was a young child attending Catholic school and church every weekend. But I had so many disconnections with religion. It seemed very fear motivated. Follow these rules, do this, don't do that. I felt the ingraining guilt and shame all along the way.

This type of religion wasn't helping me at all in this moment. And to think about it, it had never helped me. I had no connection to God, to this source of love church people talked about. I had heard all the stories. I had done all the sacraments. I went to Catholic school, but none of those things had prepared me for something like my experience. For something so painful and disorienting.

But this prayer was different. I would read it with tears streaming down my face. I would read it while yelling at God. How am I supposed to be an instrument of peace right now?

How am I supposed to console or understand or love? I want someone to do those things for me, towards me. But even through the anger and despair, I would keep reading it. Something inside me pulled me to it. It sat on my bedside table and every day I would read it.

Lord, make me an instrument of your peace:
Where there is hatred, let me sow love;
Where there is injury, pardon;
Where there is doubt, faith;

Where there is despair, hope;
Where there is darkness, light;
Where there is sadness, joy.
O divine Master, grant that I may not so much seek
To be consoled as to console,
To be understood as to understand,
To be loved as to love,
For it is in giving that we receive,
It is in pardoning that we are pardoned,
And it is in dying that we are born to eternal life.
Amen.

EMOTIONAL ROLLERCOASTER

I didn't know how to emotionally regulate or self-soothe. My nervous system had been overwhelmed. When overwhelming emotions would show up, I felt like I was dying. All of my childhood wounds were brought to the forefront. Abandonment, unworthiness, not being good enough, rejection. I was feeling all of these things in the present moment, but their source was from long ago. I was on an emotional rollercoaster with no escape. Luckily, I had a passenger with me. Although I wanted the passenger to be my husband, my real sidekick was my therapist. I would see my psychologist frequently. She was my lifeline at the time. Our weekly appointments were the best part of my week. I could barely make it to the next week before needing a refill of emotional support.

We started to unpack a lot of the big emotions I was feeling. The anger and rage were all-consuming. All of my life I had never felt it was safe to express anger. Whenever anger would show up, I would quickly shift to sadness to cover or avoid the feeling. I think as a child it wasn't acceptable to get angry, especially as a girl. Not to discredit my parents—they did the best they could with the knowledge they had. They did what they were taught: it wasn't appropriate to show anger.

I had years of anger built up inside of me and it was all being unleashed now, like a fire-breathing dragon. A dragon I didn't know how to tame. One of the tools my therapist taught me was Emotional Freedom Technique (EFT), which is an alternative treatment for dealing with physical pain and emotional distress. I would practice EFT when I was hit with intruding images of my husband and his affair partner. EFT helped move emotions, particularly anger. It was also the gateway to self-acceptance and compassion for myself. No matter what I was feeling towards another person, I was confirming that I completely loved and accepted myself.

The second tool she gave me was meditation. I started off with two to five-minute guided meditations on the Headspace app and worked my way up to ten to twelve minutes a day. The continual practice of EFT and meditation helped daily to remove myself out of a suffering state. I used other short meditations from the Breathing Room to help me move through my emotions. Some days I would do these three-minute meditations multiple times to bring me back to a calm state. Sometimes ten times a day. One of these meditations, called the Serene Mind, helped me identify and move through whatever emotion I was feeling by regulating the amygdala and growing the hippocampus in my brain.[1,2,3,4] The amygdala and hippocampus are part of a neural network that make up the limbic system. One of their functions is handling the cognitive control of emotions, or emotional regulation and response.

Here's how it works. First you recognize the emotion such as anxiety, anger, confusion and then ask yourself if this emotion is coming from the past, the future, or the present. Then you move your attention from your frontal lobe to the temporal lobe, which is moving your attention from the front of your brain (middle of your forehead) to the middle of your brain (picture the center of your skull). And it actually worked. I would go from feeling a high level of anxiety to calm in three minutes. The continual daily practice really started to shape my brain in a new way.

I was able to calm my nervous system down and shift out of a heightened state of discomfort quickly. I wouldn't stay in upset for hours on end, and I could feel calmness and peace. A welcome reprieve from all of the daily distress.

UNCONSCIOUS MARRIAGE

At the same time we were both in individual therapy, my husband and I also started seeing a couples therapist together. She was another welcome passenger on my rollercoaster. With her we began to learn about attachment theory and relationships as we dug into our childhoods.

One of the first questions she asked was, "So how would you describe your childhood?"

To which I quickly responded, "I had a great childhood!" I grew up with a loving family in a two-parent household. I had nothing to complain about. All I had were good memories. Well, from what I could remember. My parents attended all of my sporting events and competitions, coaching me and cheering me on. They provided a loving home for my sisters and me, including family dinners each night. We had family vacations and fun-filled birthday parties. I thought the world of my parents and loved them very much. Sure, there were arguments and fights, and the odd attempt to run away from home, as most thirteen-year olds do until they realize they made a mistake and want to come home for dinner time. But I would have considered us a close family. I always felt supported and taken care of. But as I continued to talk, I could sense something was missing from what I was saying as I watched the therapist take in this information, diligently writing on her notepad.

She continued, "Did you feel like you had someone to talk to?"

"Well, we didn't really talk about our feelings that much in our house," I responded.

"Did you feel safe?"

"Hmm, most of the time. Well, actually, I was scared a lot as a kid," I continued. "And I had a lot of fears."

Then it was my husband's turn. He shared about his childhood, which was far less normal than mine. I knew a bit about his upbrining from what he shared with me, but not to this extent. It didn't include a two-parent household, consistent family dinners, or participating in athletics with his parents sitting on the sidelines. It included a lot of distress, disappointment, and loss. You see, his mom left his biological dad when he was only one year old. Abandonment was set as his baseline from a young age. His mom went on to marry his stepdad when he was four years old. This involved a move to a new city. He was raised mainly by his mom and stepdad, and only saw his biological dad for a short amount of time every year. He had three sisters, one older sister from his mom and dad, and two younger sisters from his mom and stepdad. Never really feeling like he belonged, being the only boy, he was treated differently. He had a close-ish bond with his mom but she was dealing with a lot of generational trauma herself. She came from a home with an alcoholic/recovering alcoholic father and the tragic death of a sibling when she was a child. She, like many mothers, carried this unacknowledged, unhealed trauma into her family and allowed the subconscious pattern to run as she raised her children. As a parent she could only be present with him as much as she knew how, creating an avoidant attachment for her son, the wounded boy who became my husband.

Avoidant attachment occurs when a child does not consistently receive the care and attention that they need to develop a healthy relationship with their parent or caregiver. An avoidant attachment style may cause a child to hide their feelings and become emotionally distant from their parent or caregiver.[5]

As a young mother trying to do her best, she soon developed cancer, and was sick off and on for seven years. When she was forty-two she passed away. My husband was nineteen at the time of her passing. This was a tragic loss of someone he and his siblings loved so much. I can't imagine the loss of a parent. As a kid your parents seem indestructible and invincible. Permanent loss is a hard concept to grasp. He did not receive any grief counseling after her passing. I don't think he ever really grieved the loss of his mom. Instead, he shut off part of himself to the world to protect himself from the pain that her death caused. He put up invisible walls and didn't let anyone in. Including me.

I always thought we had a good relationship and marriage. It was never perfect, but we loved each other, and we made a good team. He was my best friend. We shared our thoughts and feelings, but it was usually only on my side. It was a struggle for him ever to open up. There was intimacy but not the IN-TO-ME-YOU-SEE type of intimacy. We didn't know the oh-so-popular "v" word, vulnerability. And we definitely hadn't heard of Brene Brown yet. Thank goodness our couple-therapist shared her work with us. I think I watched her world-renowned TED talk on vulnerability twenty-five times, and I still didn't understand what it was, if I had it or if I was it. Is this like a thing you are born with? Or you are taught? Is it something you can develop? These were all of my questions at the time.

Now that everything was out on the table, there were some facts we had to face. We were in an unconscious marriage.

There is a theory in psychology that we partner with people that we have the maximum potential for our soul growth. It is called Imago. These partnerships are of divine nature. Unconsciously I chose a partner that would bring these wounds to the surface. And he did the same in choosing me.

There is vast research on attachment theory that supports this. As children we develop conditioning. This conditioning becomes our subconscious programming that runs in the background of our lives. Psychologists John Bowlby and Mary Ainsworth lead the way in the area of early emotional bonds, as well as researchers Rudolph Schaffer and Peggy Emerson. More recently Harville Hendrix and Helen LaKelly Hunt have contributed with their work and research into attachment theory and unconscious marriage, including their book *Getting the Love You Want*.

I partnered with an emotionally unavailable person because that is what was modeled by my mother. She had gone through her own loss before having children. Her brother was killed in a farm accident when she was nineteen years old, and she developed anxiety. She became emotionally unavailable to her children in fear of losing us. She couldn't bear another death of a loved one, let alone her own children. It caused a lot of distance between my mom and me when all I really wanted was closeness. Though she wanted to help, she wasn't equipped with these skills herself because of her own generational trauma, nor was she able to teach them to me. From this I developed an anxious attachment.

The development of an anxious attachment style is

often associated with an inconsistent parenting pattern. Sometimes, the parents will be supportive and responsive to the child's needs and emotions. At other times, they will be misattuned to the child.[5] This is usually a response to the parent's inability to be fully present.

The lack of attunement creates an anxious response in the child. Closeness is recognized as safety, and when that is inconsistent or not present at all, the child feels alone and unsafe.

It is important to note that a parenting style is usually an automatic and unrealized pattern in adults. They raise their children the same way or similarly to how they were raised.

Fast forward to adulthood. These individuals are often insecure and anxious about their own worth in a relationship, being attuned to their partner's needs, but they cannot advocate for their own needs. They often suppress their emotions, being preoccupied by their partner's emotional state.

Having a hard time with emotions as a child, I would act out because I didn't know how to express what I was feeling. The hurt and frustrations would arise and would manifest as tantrums, or I would just completely shut down. I unconsciously replicated these behaviors in my relationships and marriage. Overwhelmed with anger or hurt, my nervous system would be flooded and I would shut down.

My husband responded to my anxiousness with avoidance because to him closeness didn't feel safe. The more anxious I was, the further away he wanted to be. We were in a dysfunctional square dance and didn't even know it. We needed to learn a new dance. We needed our old marriage to die, for a new marriage to emerge. And I had to grieve the loss of this old marriage, to create a new partnership, a new relationship.

This was as difficult as grieving a death. This marriage was all I ever knew, but I could not go back to it. It was a difficult space to be in. I couldn't imagine a new marriage with him because I didn't know what that looked like. The way ahead was all new to me, but I did believe that I could try. I would commit to learning, growing, and changing. I would commit to this new marriage, even though I couldn't see what it looked like at the time.

As I started to understand all this information from our therapist, I started to find compassion for my husband. For his experiences as a child and for him as an adult. I felt new levels of empathy and forgiveness start to bubble up. I knew I wanted to forgive him, but I just didn't know how. At least this was a start. I continued praying prayers for forgiveness towards him.

I realized when my perspective started to shift towards my husband, I could relate to his hurt and pain. It reflected the hurt and pain I had inside myself. Here were two people that really didn't love themselves very much, trying to love one another. All of these years I thought I had self-love. But deep down I wasn't being kind to myself or gentle or compassionate to myself. I participated in negative self-talk. I didn't put my needs first or forgive myself when I messed up. I had been rejecting myself since I was a young child. I really didn't love myself.

I began to wonder, Where did this self-rejection start? I was bullied a lot in school. Back in the 1980s there wasn't a term for it yet, but these days we would call it bullying. I was made fun of for having a space between my two front teeth. (That was before Madonna made it cool.) It was a sizeable space that could fit a sunflower seed. I also sucked my thumb well into elementary school, which caused a lot of teasing and name calling. So, making friends didn't come too easily. And even the friends I did have would sometimes join in with the bullying crowd, depending on the day. It was a lonely time, a confusing time. As a child having your so-called friends reject you, to go along with the cool crowd, is pretty heartbreaking. Going through these troubling years as a young child, I was learning to reject myself. I was telling myself that I was the problem. That I was not good enough.

I didn't realize it, but I was forming a program that would run in the background throughout my life. A self-betraying behavior such as self-rejection is harmful in so many ways. If you see yourself as not enough, you are bound to reflect that in all of your relationships. Always feeling less than your partner, let's say. Or undeserving of their love. And it isn't only in romantic partnerships that the underlying program will run. It will go with you, traveling with you like an invisible backpack, to your jobs, friendships, and family. We choose a job with a toxic boss. We settle for a role that is below our skill level, because we think we aren't good enough for the higher position. Or we keep friends that consistently let us down.

The only way to ditch that backpack is to first become

aware you are wearing it. Second, you have to open it up and unpack it. Some other common items in the backpack are unworthiness, shame, fear of abandonment, and insecurity. This isn't a fun process. Most of us think we are carrying around an invisible backpack full of unicorns and cotton candy, containing only things that are light, fluffy, and pretty. Let me tell you, the difficult things that developed us are not shiny and light They are going to be bumpy and rough. But they are part of us.

Kind of like how a pearl starts out as a grain of sand inside an oyster shell. It is brown, dull, and rough. And as the waves come and go, the sand in the water starts to smooth out the bumps and the brown soon turns to an iridescent glow. No one wants a grain of sand; they want the pearl. But there is a process to get there. Without the sand, there is no pearl.

Once you can see these parts of you, and they move from your subconscious to your conscious awareness, they can no longer hold power over you. You can start to override the old programming and create new thoughts about them.

For example, you pull out unworthiness to look at first. You can ask yourself: Do I have a sense of high self-worth? How do I talk to myself? Do I rely on others to validate how I feel about myself? And if your answers are not very positive, you can be curious and ask yourself why. In my case, my "why" came down to when I was a child and other kids told me I wasn't worthy. I wasn't worthy of their friendship. I wasn't worthy because of how I looked.

Next, you can use self-validating behavior to create new thoughts about your answers. An example of this could be:

"Just because I was told I wasn't worthy when I was a child doesn't mean it is true." Or, "Even though my friends didn't stick up for me, it doesn't mean I am not good enough." You can use self-empowering phrases like this to create your own self-worth.

We are a whole. We can't deny parts of ourselves because they aren't perfect. We can only function as a whole. Not parts. So, after we look at all these rough parts of ourselves, we no longer have to carry them in a backpack because they have been integrated into us.

This process doesn't happen overnight. It takes work and awareness each and every day.

But it is worth it to bring them out into the light.

Job 12:22   *He reveals the deep things of darkness and brings utter darkness into the light.*

Slowly I took each item out and looked at it. This required compassion and patience. It required holding myself both gently and fiercely. Telling my "little me" who took on this heavy backpack all by herself: "I am here now." Letting her know that I would no longer leave her alone. Through this process of unpacking, I slowly, though still defiant, started to develop self-acceptance. I started to accept all the parts of me, the positive and the negative.

I was learning this internal battle had to be won through compassion and not strength. As I started to collect these tools for healing, the self-compassion would start to increase and the self-hatred would lessen. These were small reprieves but at least it was a start.

I felt like I was learning so much, but it was exhausting. If we were going to get to the bottom of all of this, I knew I had to go deeper. We had to change the dance. But I didn't know the new steps yet and I didn't feel like my husband even wanted to learn them. I couldn't shake the feeling that he was still dancing with someone else.

I didn't know if it was my PTSD and anxiety coming up from the initial discovery of the affair or if he was still in the lie. Still in the affair.

PART THREE

My Brutiful Frenemy Self-Betrayal

IT'S NOT ME, IT'S YOU

All this time I was focused on how I was betrayed; I couldn't see the underlying truth of how I had been betraying myself for the past thirty-five years. Self-betrayal is a disconnection to self. It is living out of alignment with who you truly are. And at its worst, it is self-hatred.

It is my belief we most commonly betray ourselves in relationships out of what we think is love, by trying to give the other person what they want, when in fact it is not in alignment with our desires. This is not love, this is betrayal, slowly eroding our sense of self through our efforts to be chosen and good enough. The desire to be loved becomes stronger than loving ourselves. And this starts at a very young age with our primary caregivers, so take it easy on yourself if you are just discovering this now. (More on this in Part Seven when I discuss generational trauma.) And then we continue to search for this love into adulthood, taking from people whom we think will help us feel good inside. Taking what they truly don't want to give, but they too are searching for the very same thing. So they take from you. We become entangled in relationships, creating intertwining vines of resentment, criticism, and disconnection. So how do we unwind these vines? We learn how to connect to ourselves. We learn how to love ourselves, so that we no longer need to take. So we don't need to betray ourselves.

We use tools like meditation, mindfulness, prayer, and contemplation. We stop using external noise to distract us from what we are feeling. We sit down. We take a nap. We don't fill our schedules each day with activities and work and to-do lists. We rest. We simplify.

As I sat across the chair from my husband in the therapist's office each week, I would listen quietly as my husband shared his thoughts and feelings. Secretly judging and finger pointing. I was the one betrayed. He was the problem, not me. We were there for his issues, not mine.

Ok, let's be honest. I can't be alone here. No one wants to look at themselves. We want to blame others for our problems, right? We don't want to admit anything is wrong with us or that we have any faults.

Self-betrayal showed up for me as saying yes to something when I wanted to say no. Not keeping promises to myself. Withholding the truth, in fear of creating conflict or being abandoned. I people-pleased and suffered from perfectionism. Self-betrayal pairs well with codependency, of which I was also a culprit. I didn't know how to implement boundaries, or advocate for my own needs. I put my husband's needs and feelings ahead of my own. I abandoned myself by over-giving to prove my worth and value.

I tried to be the woman I thought he wanted, essentially losing all of who I truly was. The constructs society placed upon me were starting to crumble. The search for myself began.

Everything was stripped away from me. I was left not knowing who I was, or who my husband was; nothing made sense to me.

This led me to a very important question. Who was I? The trail of breadcrumbs continued, and I came upon Victor E. Frankl, and his book *Man's Search for Meaning*. Frankl was a neurologist, psychiatrist, and Holocaust survivor. Something he said stood out to me. "When we are no longer able to change a situation, we are challenged to change ourselves." So that is what I did.

When I asked the question, "Who am I?" I honestly didn't know. Am I my name, Andrea? Am I my job, a designer? Am I my role, a wife and mother? I didn't have a clear sense of self. And I don't know if I ever did.

I started to learn about suffering versus pain. I learned that you could be in pain, but suffering was a choice. Suffering comes from the thoughts you create about the pain you are experiencing. I was grasping for someone to fix the deep pain within. For someone to save me.

Little did I know, everything I needed to heal lay within myself.

The ability to change my internal world when my external situation was in chaos was the most powerful key to begin healing from the pain that came through infidelity.

Frankl developed a concept that he called logotherapy

while he was confined in concentration camps. It is based on the premise that the primary motivational force of an individual is to find meaning in life.[1]

According to Frankl, "We can discover this meaning in life in three different ways: (1) by creating a work or doing a deed; (2) by experiencing something or encountering someone; and (3) by the attitude we take toward unavoidable suffering" and that "everything can be taken from a man but one thing: the last of the human freedoms—to choose one's attitude in any given set of circumstances."[2]

The following list of tenets represents basic principles of logotherapy:

- Life has meaning under all circumstances, even the most miserable ones.
- Our main motivation for living is our will to find meaning in life.
- We have freedom to find meaning in what we do, and what we experience, or at least in the stance we take when faced with a situation of unchangeable suffering.[3]

He believed that a person is "capable of resisting and braving even the worst conditions." In doing so, a person can detach from situations and themselves, choose an attitude about themselves, and determine their own determinants, thus shaping their own character and becoming responsible for themselves.[3]

I wanted to learn more about suffering and freedom from

it. The founders of the Breathing Room, Sri Preethaji and Sri Krishnaji, are also the founders and teachers of Ekam, a world-renowned center for transformation and enlightenment in India. The basis of their teachings is there are only two states of being, a suffering state and a beautiful state. You are either in one or the other; there is no third state. A suffering state could be sadness, anger, depression, guilt, or even boredom. A beautiful state could be peace, calm, joy, or bliss.

When you are in a suffering state, you can only see, feel, and create chaos. You cannot solve problems, be creative, or feel the other. When you are in a beautiful state, you can see, feel, and create harmony. You can see solutions, tap into creativity, and feel another's pain.

With the help of my therapist and engaging with the practices taught by Sri Preethaji and Sri Krishnaji, I was able to detach from my husband's actions of infidelity. I chose a different attitude about myself. I started to take responsibility for myself, and to learn how to no longer be a victim. And most importantly, I discovered the suffering was coming from inside of me, not from anything outside of me. Not from what anyone else was doing or saying or how they were acting. It had nothing to do with anyone else.

I started to share a different narrative with my friends and family. I stopped repeating the old story of "My husband had an affair." That I was betrayed. That something happened to me. I started to say we had been in an unconscious marriage and an affair was an outcome of that.

Society tends to create a perpetrator and a victim in scenarios like this. I think this helps people make sense of a situation. We like to assign blame because we like certainty. And I think it is part of human nature to blame. In this case it is true that my husband had an affair, but it is also true we were in an unconscious marriage. There was a bigger picture to be seen.

Shifting out of a victim's place, to a place of empowerment and responsibility is an essential step of healing from infidelity. From this new perspective, I could also step into my power. It is easy being a victim. It is comfortable. It is familiar. You feel a false sense of control. But it is when you step out of being a victim that you find where your true power lies.

Sorry to break it to you, society, but you will have to look elsewhere for your victim, because there ain't no victim here!

Ok, ok, all well and good in theory. But how do you actually shift from being a victim?

Here are a few ways. You can start taking ownership of your wants and needs. Don't rely on others to make it happen: create it yourself. And say no to things that you don't want to do. Let go of people-pleasing and choose for yourself.

Second, get curious about the underlying feelings of powerlessness you experience. Stop blaming others for how you feel and make changes that will make yourself feel good. You have the power to change your life to what you would like it to be. Third, create boundaries, become reliable, and then hold yourself accountable.

Boundaries will help you define your identity, help you take responsibility for your life, and release yourself from painful emotions like anger and resentment. Being reliable and accountable are also necessary in building this empowered identity. If you make a promise to yourself, keep it. And lastly, be kind to yourself. This last one is easier said than done.

I felt so much hatred towards myself. Although I was starting to learn, I really didn't know how to be compassionate and hold myself gently. As I became more grounded in my body and calm in my mind, I became aware that any feeling I felt toward my husband was also towards myself, so faith and compassion were the only way out.

The level of compassion we have for another reflects the level of compassion we have for ourselves. We are all connected. When we feel disdain, anger, or hatred towards another, we are also feeling those emotions about ourselves. When we start to feel compassion towards ourselves, we then are able to give that gift to another.

My therapist gave me ideas on how to help others: volunteering, doing acts of kindness, or just donating to the food bank. There are studies that show people who help others while they are suffering recover more quickly. Helping others regulate their emotions helps us regulate our own emotions, decreases symptoms of depression, and ultimately, improves our emotional well-being.[4]

She also had me create a gratitude journal. She encouraged me to write down five things I was thankful for every day, even when things seemed to not be going my way. There was always something to be thankful for. This helped me see the joyful things that happened and to look beyond the uncertainty and sorrow I felt. There was a huge hole in my heart, and it would take a while to heal. While it was healing,

I needed to believe that one day I would feel free of the pain. I needed to believe it before I would see it. Gratitude is one way to put yourself in this place of praise. Praise for what is. Praise for what is to come.

This is easier said than done. I tried to be consistent, but some days I didn't have anything to write. I was just so angry and had so much hurt inside. It was hard to access gratitude all the time. I tried to remind myself I was doing the best that I could. There were many days when I would just go and eat a donut so later in the day I could maybe feel grateful for that donut.

I had reminders that would tell me I needed to act before I felt. So, I needed to write things down before I felt like doing so. However small, there would be something to write down. These reminders came from my therapist, podcasts, meditation, or books I was reading. This reoccurring message would consistently pop up.

There is a story in the Bible about the prophet Elijah living through three years of drought: the land saw no rain. Crops and cattle died. The people desperately needed rain. But what they needed more than rain was God. God wanted to show them the truth, so he told Elijah to pray for rain and declare its impending arrival. Elijah obeyed. He was thankful for the rain before it came. He believed and felt its arrival before the first drop fell.

Another verse that shows this beautiful see-it-before-you-believe-it faith is in Hebrews.

> Hebrews 11:1-4 *Now faith is confidence in what we hope for and assurance about what we do not see. This is what the ancients were commended for. By faith we understand that the universe was formed at God's command, so that what is seen was not made out of what was visible.*

HEALING TRAUMA

Another modality for healing I used with one of my therapists was Eye Movement Desensitization and Reprocessing, or EMDR.[5] EMDR is a form of psychotherapy in which the person being treated recalls distressing experiences while doing bilateral stimulation, such as side-to-side eye movement or tapping either side of the body. It is an effective treatment for people that suffer from anxiety, PTSD, and trauma. This process helps by reconnecting the traumatized person in a safe and measured way to the images, self-thoughts, emotions, and body sensations associated with the trauma, and allowing the natural healing powers of the brain to move toward adaptive resolution.[6]

It is based on the idea that symptoms occur when trauma and other negative or challenging experiences overwhelm the brain's natural ability to heal, and that the healing process can be facilitated and completed through bilateral stimulation while the client is re-experiencing the trauma in the context of the safe environment of the therapist's office. This is known as dual awareness. Over time, exposure to traumatic memories will no longer induce negative feelings and distressing symptoms.[6]

The trauma of the discovery of the affair had left me with PTSD symptoms. I experienced intruding images of my husband and his partner. They showed up during the day and at night. They were all-consuming. The breach of trust had left me flailing. I was left not knowing what was true and what wasn't. For the first few months after the affair began I didn't know who the other woman was. I would have anxiety about running into her downtown or at a coffee shop. She could be anyone, so any woman became a suspect. It was an unsettling feeling. I was also anxious about my husband's whereabouts and activities at all times. The recurring thoughts left me feeling retraumatized daily. I was hyper-vigilant, and it was exhausting.

The weekly sessions with EMDR slowly started to help and the distress would lessen.

I would put on headphones that would have instrumental music playing, alternating from one ear to the other. Then my therapist and I would discuss the thoughts and topics that were distressing at the time. As the tears flowed and anger roared, I could feel the tension lessen in my body. I could feel the return to safety. A welcome reprieve.

Along with EMDR, my therapist and I would simultaneously use Somatic Experiencing therapy.

She would guide me while we talked about where in my body I would feel certain sensations. She helped me to develop an increased tolerance for difficult bodily sensations and suppressed emotions, addressing the root cause of the trauma symptoms related to the infidelity. We would talk about an upsetting issue and then the sensation in my body would lesson each time. I was releasing stored emotions from my body. And with her help, we started to heal my nervous system at the same time. It is all connected.

Somatic Experiencing was developed by Peter A. Levine. This approach releases traumatic shock, which is key to transforming PTSD and the wounds of emotional and early developmental attachment trauma. It offers a framework to assess where a person is stuck in the fight, flight or freeze responses and provides clinical tools to resolve these fixated physiological states.[7]

Dr. Levine was inspired to study stress on the animal nervous system when he realized that animals are constantly under threat of death yet show no symptoms of trauma. What he discovered was that trauma has to do with the third survival response to perceived life threat, which is freeze. When fight and flight are not options, we freeze and immobilize, like playing dead. This makes us less of a target. However, this reaction is time-sensitive; in other words, it needs to run its course, and the massive energy that was prepared for fight or flight gets discharged through shakes and trembling. If the immobility phase doesn't complete, then that charge stays trapped, and, from the body's perspective, it is still under threat. The Somatic Experiencing method works to release this stored energy and turn off the threat alarm that causes severe dysregulation and dissociation.[7]

Even with months of sessions with Somatic Experiencing

Therapy, I continued to have unrelenting pain under my one rib. At first, I thought I might have a rib out of place from the pregnancy. But it didn't seem to stop after my daughter was born, and now I was about three months postpartum. I made an appointment with my family doctor and had an x-ray but the doctors couldn't find anything wrong. I had been going to acupuncture prior during my pregnancy and thought it wouldn't hurt to try it again.

I explained the pain to my acupuncturist, and he started to explain to me how the body stores anger in the liver. This was the exact spot where my pain was. He helped me release the shock and anger I had, a little bit each appointment. He would put the needles in, and I would be lying on the bed overcome with emotion. I would just start sobbing. After a few weeks of appointments, the pain under my rib started to subside. It was amazing. It took a few months of treatments for the pain to be fully gone. But this added benefit of releasing the shock of the infidelity and the deep feelings of anger really helped me.

I continued therapy, EMDR, and Somatic Experiencing. I continued to heal. I used acupuncture to help release the anger, sadness, and hurt. I continued to heal. I prayed, meditated, and made an effort to be grateful every day. I continued to heal a little bit day after day.

BAPTISM BY FIRE

Darkness lift your heavy veil,
For one will come before you,
To lift your stronghold,
Free your tattered soul,
And set you free.

Luke 3:16   *John answered them all, "I baptize you with water. But one who is more powerful than I will come, the straps of whose sandals I am not worthy to untie. He will baptize you with the Holy Spirit and fire."*

A baptism by fire could be described as a fiery trial of faith that endures suffering while purifying the faithful who look upon God and are transformed, not consumed. Well, I definitely felt like I was being consumed at the time. All I felt was pain. But there was nowhere else to go. I had to stand in the fire with the pain.

I didn't know that all the while I was being transformed, I was being forged in the fire.

The months continued to go by like molasses. The first few months after you give birth are usually the hardest in normal circumstances. Sleep deprived and exhausted, you are stuck in a cycle of feeding and changing diapers. To say I was feeling worn down would be an understatement. I had a fine balance of hope and despair; either could tip the scale depending on the day.

We were nearing Thanksgiving now and my husband was still stuck in his own dark internal world. There had been some progress made in our therapy, but it felt like there was such a long way to go. Thanksgiving Day came and the rollercoaster took yet another unexpected turn. Overwhelmed by his internal torment of guilt and shame I am sure, my husband came to me and said he was still in the affair. That hadn't ended. And he finally revealed who the affair partner was.

My intuitive feelings were right all along. I knew deep down it was her. And I knew deep down it hadn't ended.

The wound that I was trying so hard to begin to mend was quickly broken open, fresh as the day of the initial discovery. Ripped open even deeper this time.

I don't know why, but I didn't react. I didn't yell or scream or even cry. I just stood there and held him as he wept in my arms. He had said how sorry he was and that he couldn't lie to me any longer. I think looking back at this now, he was breaking up with me at that moment. His tears were genuine. Just like in any breakup, there is a sense of loss. And in his heart he knew what was coming next.

Strangely I felt a sense of relief. Ok, I thought, now it will be over. Now we can start to repair.

"You need to call her right now and tell her it is over," I said, "You need to put your family first."

He called her and they were breaking up right in front of me. I could hear her crying on the other side of the phone. I was dictating what to say to her.

I will never forget the sound of his voice. He had never spoken like that to me. In that compassionate, loving tone. I felt like an outsider. I knew he was far gone in that moment. That he really loved her.

He hung up the phone, but it didn't feel resolved.

As we talked it became clear that he wanted to stay with her. That he didn't want to end the affair. It took every ounce of strength in my body and soul to remain calm. I used my tools had learned so far and called my therapist. She helped regulate my nervous system and I went to sleep upstairs while he went to the basement.

We both wanted what was best for our children, one who was still only four months old, and we agreed to be separated but live in the same house. We had been learning in therapy that the years from birth to two and a half are the most critical years in a child's life for forming attachment with both parents.

He moved into the basement, and I created an agreement of what this living arrangement would look like, creating a schedule for when he could spend time with the kids. I knew this wouldn't be easy, but I wanted to know I did everything I could to see if our marriage could survive in the end, even if we were separated for this period of time. I thought perhaps I could outrun the affair.

Being separated in the same house was weird and awful. It was as if ten years of a meaningful relationship was distilled down to mere acquaintances in the blink of an eye. That it all meant nothing. That none of the past years were real. I was losing my husband and my best friend all at the same time. Every inside joke, gone. Every hug, gone. Every moment of laughter, gone.

The house that was filled with so much joy, love, laughter, and warmth quickly turned sterile and cold. We no longer shared meals together. We didn't talk inside the house, only at our therapy sessions together that we had each week. Separate spaces, separate lives, one house.

The only thing we still shared were our kids. And even that time was starting to be divided and experienced separately.

We both wanted to be the best parents we could be for our children, and I could still provide him with that opportunity. I remember the nights, waking up to feed the baby then texting him to come up and put her back to sleep. He wanted to still help; even though this isn't how I wanted it to be, I allowed him to help. After all she was only four months old, and we learned from therapy this bonding time with both parents was so essential.

I longed for us to just be all together. To be parenting together. I would fall asleep crying most nights. Plagued with migraines caused by the intense anger I still had. I would hold a rosary my grandmother gave me years ago and keep it under my pillow. I thought about my grandma and how she must have felt when she lost her son in the farm accident when he was nineteen. The grief. The sorrow. The anger. I would talk to her in the still of the night. She had passed away, but I still found comfort in speaking to her. I find it is a bit like praying, talking to someone that has passed away.

I remember watching my grandma praying the rosary when I was little. I decided to start praying the Hail Mary prayer I learned when I was younger. I already had it memorized.

I would think about Mary as I said her prayer. I was so mad at God. I just wanted my old life back. I wondered if Mary thought that at all.

Well, spoiler alert, she didn't. I looked it up to be sure. Yeah, in fact, if you can believe it, she does the opposite. When the angel Gabriel visits her to tell her that she will become pregnant and give birth to a son whom they will call Jesus, the Son of God, she gladly accepts.

I wondered, How did Mary know how to do this? How did she know to accept and praise?

Was she taught that as a child? Did she learn it in school? Who told her to do these things? How did it come easy to her? Or maybe it wasn't easy for her, but she decided to do it anyways.

Or maybe she just had a feeling that accepting *what was* was pivotal in God's plan, no matter how uncertain she felt.

I was stuck in this place of in-between. I couldn't go back, and I couldn't go forward. I didn't know what the future would be. Us together or Us apart. I hated it. This place of in-between became my norm. I was stuck in this stupid house, with someone I was supposed to be married with, but we were no longer acting like we were married. To have this relationship be reduced to mere acquaintances was so painful.

Being forced to stay in the "stupid" house together was a blessing in disguise for me in a sense, as it allowed for deep healing to occur within me. Healing that I am not sure would have been able to take place if not having to endure this uncomfortable time together in the same space. Being in this in-between place, I knew I had to adapt and change, or I would be miserable.

My therapist started to talk to me about anticipatory grief, as she could see I was moving into that state. With my husband's constant changes in mind and heart, it wasn't allowing me to proceed through this grieving process entirely, which is somewhat chaotic. (Remembering that the old marriage had to die for a new one to emerge.)

She shared with me a book on this called *Anticipatory Grief: Expecting the Loss, Feeling the Pain* by Marty Hogan. This book offers ways to cope with these painful, confusing feelings. Being in this state of grief means that we are grieving a loss before the loss has happened.

Reading the book and completing the journal prompts helped me to grieve. It helped me make sense of the conflicting feelings of hope and despair I was having. It helped me to grieve the old marriage, the old versions of Us. I was preparing for the loss. The loss of my best friend. The loss of my husband.

I started reading about acceptance. Here is what I found. Acceptance doesn't mean liking, wanting, choosing, or supporting something that happened or that you are experiencing. But by struggling against the pain, we create undue suffering. The pain might be there, but we can alleviate some of the suffering. Recognizing that you can't change the nature of this exact moment, and accepting that recognition reduces the pain around the subject, creating less stress, anxiety and producing a sense of calmness.[8]

Maybe I should try to be more like Mary. If I was going to be in a place of uncertainty, maybe I could make it more tolerable. Maybe I could move into a place of acceptance. And maybe even experience joy. I didn't know how I would do it but I just started to try.

I started to take actions that made the acceptance of this situation easier. I set boundaries that there would no longer be family meals. That if we were separated, we would do things separately with the kids. That he would be responsible for his own laundry, cleaning, and sharing household duties that I used to take care of. I moved his things out of our bedroom and bathroom, into his own room. I created a physical distinction of the internal distinction I was making while I grieved.

This process was so hard. I didn't want to do it, but I knew I had to. Packing up his clothes and personal items was one of the hardest things to do. Each item held so many memories. I started to take down our wedding and family photos throughout the house. Holding them tightly, remembering the moments as I looked at each one before putting them into a chest. They held so much happiness, but also so much pain.

And when the heartache and pain was too much to bear alone, I had wonderful friends that came over. They brought dinners. A listening ear. Even just coming over so I could take a nap. They brought their presence which was enough for me. Just to have someone sit in the pain with you in silence is sometimes all that is needed.

And luckily, I have amazing parents and they came to stay with us regularly to help with meals, the kids, and taking care of the house. And to support me more importantly, emotionally, during this complicated time. Bless their hearts because they had to find their own strength and forgiveness to share a home with their son-in-law that was seeing another woman. I mean, can you wrap your head around that? God was working in more ways than one.

My dad was in a push and pull dynamic with his anger and empathy towards my husband.

At one point Dad did tell my husband that he could go to a homeless shelter because he was so upset with his behavior. The pull of his anger won the battle that day. But there were also moments of compassion, like my dad cleaning and setting up the bedroom in the basement so my husband could have a more livable and enjoyable space to stay.

My parents were going through a grieving process of their own. Letting go of a son-in-law they had loved for eight years. The hurt he caused me with the affair had hurt everyone, the whole family. It was in a sense a betrayal for them too. They had trusted him and loved him too. The debris of the destruction from the infidelity reached far past just myself.

PART FOUR

Doping Out on Facebook

SOME HOLY SHIT

Then came the day of my great realization in that church service. Holy shit! I thought, I am Leah! I am the other woman. I feel unloved, worthless, and rejected. I was cast aside.

I sat there bawling in my seat as I continued to listen. Although Leah longed for love and union with another, God wanted her to become connected to him first, emotionally and spiritually. Years later, Leah delivered her fourth child, Judah, which meant "praise." An unloved, rejected, and disappointed woman finally decided it was time to praise God and confess out loud, be thankful and find her joy in him.

Then another thought came. Remember Leah's second child was named Simeon? Holy shit! My second child is named Simone, the one born during conflict and chaos. We never knew the meaning of her name when we chose it, but it means "hearkening" or "One who hears". This is some real Holy shit right here.

Leah's worth was tied to Jacob and she was trying to earn his love by giving him children. When really, she was whole as herself. I had been seeking external validation my whole life. My worth lay outside of myself too.

Ok, so if my worth was outside of me, where was it?

INSTAGRAM GOD

In the quest to find this valuable possession, I had to start where my worth was hidden at the time. One of the places it was hiding was within social media. So, I made the decision to quit all social media. I deleted my accounts and apps off my phone. As a millennial ingrained in this online world, it came as quite a challenge. But being in such a stressful situation I needed to start keeping stock of what was helping me and what was not. I was already drowning in judgment, shame, and comparison, and I was finding social media starting to have a negative effect on my mental health. I found it would only cause me more suffering for the pain I was in. I did what was best for the highest good of all, protecting myself, my children, and my husband.

During that year I made personal growth my full-time job, alongside tending to my newborn and preschooler. The time I would have been wasting on social media was being used to gain wisdom and strength through reading, meditation, podcasts, and therapy sessions. My world at the time was a shade of grey (and not the fifty shades kind) and the thought of colourful images of happy families, celebrations, and milestones only triggered more pain. I also realized I couldn't post about being a happy family of four when everything around me was falling apart. It would be inauthentic of me to show that things were fine when they were not. I didn't have the energy to put up a facade, nor did I want to.

Research shows that it takes on average sixty-six days to change a habit.[1] I found that to be true for me. After a month I started to become used to this change. And each month it got easier and easier. By the third month I began to feel free. I didn't need it anymore. I wasn't tied to my phone; in fact, I was hardly on it. I started filling my days with inspiration from thoughtful writers, philosophers, and spiritual leaders. I began a gratitude journal and practiced meditation.

At the same time, I downloaded the YouVersion Bible app on my phone. I started reading plans on forgiveness, anger, strength, and courage, each day replacing the time I would have spent on Instagram with time reading devotionals and passages from the Bible. I was learning how other individuals had overcome their own hardships and started to learn that strength and resilience can be found inside all of us. I grew in my faith and in closeness to God. I started looking forward to starting my day off this way. I would spend fifteen to thirty minutes every morning sitting in this safe place. Just me and God. It was a source of healing, growth, and grace.

I started to become more aware of my surroundings. I was present. I was available. I was evolving. I thought I was staying connected by being on social media, but as time passed in the offline world, I started to feel more connected than I ever have. Connected to myself, to God, and my internal world. At the same time connecting to my external world in an authentic way.

I was more available to my daughters. Available to experience joy, gratitude, and love in real time. Not by capturing it in a photo or video to share with friends. I felt those moments deeply in my soul. I felt free of judgment and comparison as a mother. I didn't feel this heavy pressure of trying to keep up with other moms whom I thought were doing it better than me. Whose kids looked more put together than mine. I was able to release the wound of perfectionism carried from childhood, letting my older daughter come into her own creative being rather than presenting her as photoshoot-ready every day.

Connections with strangers came frequently. At shops, cafes, and restaurants. Rather than sitting with my head down on my phone, I was engaging in new conversations with people. Real people. I noticed and became aware of how many of us are stuck in this head-down posture, obsessing over what filter to use or heading down a rabbit hole of this addictive selfie-generated society.

One of the biggest realizations I had as I look back on my experience is that I could have used social media to distract, avoid, or cover up the pain I was in. But I didn't. And I am so grateful for that. The longer you avoid pain, the longer it takes to heal. I know that some of where I am at today is partially credited to stepping back from this online society social club.

My mental health thanked me. My daughters thanked me. My evolved self thanked me. I don't think the personal growth I have achieved over this past year could have been accomplished while being on social media. The departure created the space I needed to learn and grow.

Social media has the potential to be such a positive influence when you start to be mindful of who you follow and what content you allow in. When you start to be more mindful of the content you post and ask yourself what kind of impact you want to make. When you start to ask yourself, Is this making me feel good or not? Am I seeking validation, worthiness, or acceptance? Am I judging another? For when you judge another, you are in turn judging yourself and causing yourself harm as well. I found that the false validation I received from it was stripping away my true sense of self. I would start to ask myself, Does it make it more valid if I share this with others? Or am I doing this for myself?

As the search continued, I started to become aware of another place my worth was hidden. In my marriage. And in my husband. I started to ask myself questions like, Who am I if I am not a wife? What is it about being married? What kind of belonging does it provide for me? Belonging to someone? That is so messed up, if you think about it. There is a sense of security that comes with being married. That you are theirs, and they are yours.

I think I finally felt like I belonged in my life where I felt for so long as an outsider. It felt comforting and safe. It felt like something I always longed for.

There is so much fake news around marriage and love. Disney, romantic comedies, patriarchal history, the list goes on and on. As kids we see these movies and hear stories of princesses and princes, and I think it just sets us up for failure as adults. We see these unrealistic expectations of what marriage and love are.

The other night as I was putting my oldest daughter to bed, she asked me, "Mom, how old do you have to be to get married?"

I responded, "Well legally eighteen, but it is up to you. You can be twenty-five, thirty-five, fifty." I went on to tell her that she didn't have to be in a rush or get married at all. I told her that there is so much she will want to do. In my own selfishness I told her to wait until she is at least thirty.

I then asked her why. She said that in all the movies, the people getting married look young. I told her that is true, they do look young. And those movies aren't really accurate. She fell asleep contently.

I remember for our wedding ceremony we had vintage handkerchiefs that we handed out. We had them custom screen printed. They read, Happily Ever After. A phrase that is at the end of every fairy tale. Why wouldn't we believe it to be the truth? Naively thinking that was it, we accepted it. We met, fell in love, and got married. We did it. Not understanding fully the work that comes with marriage. That "Happily ever after" wouldn't be something achieved because of a ceremony.

The last place my worth was hidden was within being a mother. As a mother I had duties and responsibilities, I was both needed and wanted. I started to think if I didn't have kids, would I still be needed or wanted? Being a mother provided me with a sense of identity. I was part of mom groups, attended play dates, and did all the mom things, thinking it somehow made me who I was. And God forbid I did one of those things poorly, and I wasn't up to the certain standard that was set.

I even remember noticing that when I went back to work after a year of maternity leave and my oldest daughter went to daycare, I felt like I didn't know who I was any longer. Like something was missing if she wasn't with me. I found myself hiding behind her in social situations. It was easy if I was with my kids because then people would ask about the girls. When it was just me, I felt exposed. People then wanted to ask questions about me. I was going to be seen, and it felt uncomfortable.

I knew I had to learn to stand on my own, as my own person, without the title of "mother." I knew I had to become comfortable with being seen as Andrea and not just Colette and Simone's mom. The problem was I didn't know who Andrea was. I don't know if I had ever truly known.

I had a laminated poster in my room as a child with my name on it. It said, "Andrea, she warms the world, her smile like the sun, caring for all, this kindhearted womanly one." I remember looking at it and reading that phrase often. I was looking for someone or something to tell me who I was.

I never really ever liked my name, I always wanted a cooler name, something more unique. Now I realize that it was never the name that I didn't like, it was the person. I didn't like myself very much.

I decided I would get to know her and see if I could mend this relationship with myself. I was told the way to do this was to essentially date myself. I would need to spend time by myself. I wrote a list of things I liked to do and went and did them, alone. Coffee dates, yoga, cross-country skiing, dinner dates, going to the movies, paddle boarding, you name it, I did it. I started to get to know and even like the person I was spending time with. I was starting to find belonging and fulfillment inside of myself.

And guess what? I even started to like my name. I looked up what my name meant. Andrea means "brave or courageous." Hmm. That was kind of cool. It also said it meant "manly." That one I was less excited about.

I wondered when I had started to let my worth live outside of me. Surely that didn't only start on D-day; it had to have started a long time ago. Or maybe the bigger issue was: Perhaps I had never really found it in the right place to begin with.

Not having had a close relationship with God, I was never really able to feel and understand the connection of my worth and God. That they went together. I was listening to what others said about me and not what God said about me. And no fault of my own, as I didn't even know what God said about me.

Things like these:

Psalm 139:14   *I praise you because I am fearfully and wonderfully made; your works are wonderful, I know that full well.*

---

1 John 3:1: *See what great love the Father has lavished on us, that we should be called children of God! And that is what we are! The reason the world does not know us is that it did not know him.*

I had spent a lifetime looking for my worth. Looking in friends, magazines, posters, social media, relationships, and motherhood. The only place I didn't think to look was inside. And it's not like I did this intentionally. It was happening unconsciously.

And as I started to come closer to God, and my faith increased, I could feel my sense of worth starting to grow as well. Like Leah, I had to let go of what I thought was my source of worth, to let in the true source, God. That security can never be found in a marriage or in a person.

What a relief, because I no longer had a sure thing. I no longer had the promise of a marriage. The reality was it might not work out. Lately it wasn't looking good. But I could summon up what bravery I had, let go of a lifelong search, and stop looking. Because now I knew God. And now that I knew of that type of security, worth, and love, I didn't need anything else.

BEING REAL WOMEN

Funny enough, the first group I joined at my new church was a Bible study on the book of Ruth.[2] My mentor, Pastor Jen, led me to join this group. I think that was a bit of a set-up by God. I didn't know the story of Ruth at the time, but as each week passed, I felt a strong resemblance between Naomi and me. To the pain she carried.

Naomi was a widow. She had lost her husband and both of her sons, and in that, her livelihood too. Naomi turned bitter from her losses. She even told people her name was no longer Naomi, but now it was Mara, which means bitter. Ruth was one of her daughters-in-law, whose husband had also died.

Naomi decided to return to Bethlehem where the barley harvest was beginning. She urged Ruth to stay behind, saying she could no longer be of any help for her, only a burden as a widow, no longer having any sons. Ruth was loyal and said that she would stay with Naomi.

Ruth 1:16-17   *But Ruth replied, "Don't urge me to leave you or to turn back from you. Where you go I will go, and where you stay I will stay. Your people will be my people and your God my God. Where you die I will die, and there I will be buried. May the Lord deal with me, be it ever so severely, if even death separates you and me."*

Ruth had every right to be bitter as well. To be angry at God. Her husband had died. But she remained faithful and kind, trusting God, allowing forgiveness to develop in her heart. She allowed healing in her heart. In doing so she found work in a field, which provided money and food for her and her mother-in-law Naomi. Her kindness and loyalty made such an impact with the owner, Boaz, that they got married. He then provided for both her and Naomi.

Ruth was a blessing for Naomi in a time that she needed God the most. She reflected God's love for her. And through Ruth's forgiving heart, she allowed God to bless them both.

FORGIVENESS LIKE A THAWING RIVER

As I sat on a bench on the top of a coulee in early spring, I looked down towards a small stream that was divided into two pathways. One side of the stream was frozen. The other side was partially melted, with some water flowing through. I sat and thought to myself how similar I was to the water, being presented with two options. Did I want to be the frozen side of the river? Frozen, stuck, and cold? Did I want to live with bitterness and a closed heart, like Naomi?

Or did I want to be the side of the stream that, though partially frozen, still had water flowing through? Flowing with life and warmth. Living with an open heart, like Ruth?

I decided to choose the flowing side. I decided to choose love instead of fear. I decided to choose compassion and forgiveness instead of bitterness and resentment. I decided to choose to let go with love, not anger. Though I made the choice, the water would still take a while to fully thaw, but at least it was a start.

Pain and disappointment are inevitable, but it is what you decide to do with that pain that will either define you or deliver you. Life is going to present you with circumstances and opportunities to be frozen water or flowing water. At these times, take some time for reflection and ask yourself if staying in bitterness and unforgiveness is worth your freedom. Is it worth not letting go of someone that wronged you, or lied to you, or didn't show up for you in the way you wanted? When given the opportunity for freedom, say yes. Choose love and not fear. Choose courage and compassion and let the love flow through your being. The stream will only become stronger, and the current will continue to carry you through this river of life.

What was cool about both Leah and Ruth's stories is that through their endurance of hardship and pain, they made an impact for years to come. They decided to be flowing water. They didn't allow bitterness and unforgiveness to defeat them. Instead, they chose to praise God in the midst of their troubles, trusting God had a plan when things didn't go like they planned.

They both became matriarchs landing in the family tree of Jesus. Through their faith and praise they had a generational impact. God used both of their unfavorable circumstances to produce hope and love for the world. That is pretty remarkable.

Those are some real women right there.

The thing is, I didn't know if I could be one of those women, but I was going to try.

PART FIVE

My Triathlon Year and Other Clichés

FAITH AND ENDURANCE

There is a passage in the book of James that I love and visit often.

James 1: 2-8   *Consider it pure joy, my brothers and sisters, whenever you face trials of many kinds, because you know that the testing of your faith produces perseverance. Let perseverance finish its work so that you may be mature and complete, not lacking anything. If any of you lacks wisdom, you should ask God, who gives generously to all without finding fault, and it will be given to you. But when you ask, you must believe and not doubt, because the one who doubts is like a wave of the sea, blown and tossed by the wind. That person should not expect to receive anything from the Lord. Such a person is double-minded and unstable in all they do.*

This passage holds a special place in my heart. It was one of the catalysts for diving deeper into my faith.

I was visiting my parents eight months after D-day, and the first time my husband told me he was leaving for the other woman. I was distraught. I grabbed my dried wedding bouquet from my childhood room and jumped in the car. I drove to the edge of town, got out of the car and threw my bouquet into the darkness of the field. I yelled and screamed. Tears streamed down my face. I ran and grabbed the bouquet and beat it against the ground as the flowers fell apart, disassembling and disintegrating into the dusty earth. I continued to stomp and crush any remaining flowers until nothing was left. I saw myself in the flowers. Beaten, disintegrating, disassembling until there was nothing left. I was mere dust and earth. Yet all of God's creations are formed from dust and earth.

Genesis 2:7   *And the Lord God formed man from the dust of the ground, and breathed into his nostrils the breath of life; and man became a living soul.*

I came back to the house, went into the office and opened my dad's Bible. The page with that verse in James was what my eyes landed on.

Endurance and faith go hand in hand. To endure is to bear hardship. But to endure with faith, your hardship is turned into glory. It takes grit, courage, patience, and perseverance,

PART FIVE: MY TRIATHLON YEAR AND OTHER CLICHÉS

but sign me up, because I don't want my hardships to be wasted. I want them turned into glory and used for the greater good. I want my decisions and actions to have impact for years to come.

A week went by; he came back, wanting to still try to repair. This felt like a yo-yo of emotional torture for me, but I wanted to make sure that we tried our best for our kids. I still had some fight left in me. This would be my final round in the ring. For the next few months while we continued to go to couples' therapy together, this verse continued to show up for me. These were a hard few months. When the anger and rage was so strong and wrapped so lightly around me, I would pray and meditate on releasing this anger instead of acting it out on him. We both gave it our all. He was in his own battle and trying to find direction on which way to go. We both started to realize the only two options for our lives would be to be happy together or happy apart, because that is what was best for both of us and the girls.

While he was deciding whether to stay or go, I started to swim. It was very therapeutic. Water moves energy really well, so it was a perfect place to put my anger, at the bottom of a pool. It also creates a space for conscious breathing and having to be in the present moment. This led me to train for a triathlon. I wanted to create an empowering memory on the one-year anniversary date of the discovery of the affair, whether we stayed together or not. The date was on the weekend of a local triathlon. In the same triathlon the year before I was cheering on my husband as he crossed the finish line. This year, though, I decided the triumph would be in my name.

The training did not come easy. I was a terrible swimmer. I knew how to swim to survive, not for endurance. There were times when my goggles would fill with tears, as I tried to make it across the pool. I would drag my heavy body through the water, looking down at the bottom, thinking I felt so heavy that I would just sink. Heavy with grief, anger, and shame. A voice in my head would say, Just keep going. So I kept going, one stroke at a time.

The correlation of strength and endurance in my journey through infidelity and the triathlon was a perfect example of my intestinal fortitude that was building. It is astounding really. I didn't see it at the time, but from the bird's eye view now years after, I realize that I was becoming a badass. Intestinal fortitude is having courage and endurance to go on. These characteristics were formed from the struggles and sweat I endured. The sleepless nights, the unknowing: Was he staying, was he going? Could we recover from this? What would my life be like now? How is this going to affect our beautiful girls? We were just starting our lives together as a family of four, and I didn't know if this grenade would be lethal. I made healing my full-time job, reading every book recommended by my therapists and doing daily journal exercises.

One of those books was *Living and Loving after Betrayal* by Steven Stosny. In this book he provides a compassionate self-healing guide to recovering in the aftermath of infidelity and betrayal. He includes exercises and tools to heal from betrayal, restore inner resilience, regain trust in yourself and others. The one thing I didn't realize is that when you lose trust in someone significant to you, like your husband, you lose trust in everyone. This was something that I had to really work on. The more I focused on rebuilding trust in myself, the more trust in others naturally started to follow.

The book explains that one of the most important elements in overcoming emotional pain is developing a healing identity. I used exercises to identify with my strengths and resilience instead of with thoughts of unfairness and blame. It is natural to have these hurtful thoughts for a length of time and sometimes even feel overwhelmed by them. But with maintaining a healing identity, you will be able to resist the impulse to focus and magnify them, bringing you out of that victim mentality quickly. A healing identity is responsible and powerful. It also frees up all of your mental, emotional, and spiritual resources for healing and growth.

Another strong recurring element from the book is self-compassion. Stonsy shares that compassion is the best psychological defense you can have. The alternates: resentment, withdrawal, or aggression. Compassion protects you and others and prevents future hurt by:

- Restoring core values, which lowers the effect of others on your value or adequacy.
- Rarely invoking anger in others, keeping destructive defenses at bay.
- Offering protection from the pain of betrayed trust.

Self-compassion is a sympathetic response to your hurt, distress, or vulnerability, with a motivation to heal, repair and improve. It is empowering and gives you the sense that you can make your life better. Through these exercises I started to see that the level of compassion I could hold for myself was a direct reflection of compassion I could hold for another. Anger and resentment started to shift into compassion and grace for my husband.

WHILE IT WAS STILL DARK

I started attending my new church in January 2019. Each week I remember hearing all of these new worship songs that I really connected to. It was so refreshing. The most exciting song from the Catholic church I attended growing up was Joy to the World! And that was only at Christmas. Normal Sundays were hymns that made no sense to me and hardly classified as a song. I was deeply moved by these new songs, singing about "Another in the Fire" with me, and being "Surrounded." That God was fighting my battles for me. I would sway back and forth and tears would fall down my face. I was singing the words to release the sadness and pain from my soul. I could feel God's presence envelop me. He would say to me, Give me your fears and anxiety. Trust in me. Don't act out of anger. I will give you rest.

Each week the sermons spoke to me directly, it was like they were crafted directly for me. I couldn't believe it. I looked forward to Sunday' and the healing that would occur in the listening, in the swaying and singing. There was one sermon that stood out. It was an Easter message. It really described how I was feeling over the past year.

The core scripture was:

| John 20:1 | *Early on Sunday morning, while it was still dark, Mary Magdalene came to the tomb and found that the stone had been rolled away from the entrance.* |

The key to this verse for me was, "While it was still dark." While it was dark, there was something else happening that I couldn't see because of the darkness I was in. I couldn't see what God was doing in my life at the time because of the heartbreak and hopelessness that I felt, but He was still there working.

While I feared the future, God was setting me free from the past, from betrayal and disappointment. While I was feeling defeated and not good enough, something new was about to be born. Because while it is dark, God does his best work. What looked like death was a resurrection. I believe Jesus' resurrection shows us that we can be reborn. In every situation there can be rebirth. In every darkness there can be new life. In every challenge, trial, and loss, light will emerge if you let it. How do you let the light emerge? You say, Thy kingdom come, thy will be done on earth as it is in heaven. You ask to see things differently. Show me a new perspective. Ask for a miracle. And through that, our challenges, trials, and loss are used to show others who God is.

If this was a screenplay for a rom com, here would be the part where I would tell you we were able to rebuild and miraculously survive the damage that occurred. But this is the final round, folks, and it ends with a knockout. A face on the canvas kind of blow. You know the kind where the fighter stays down, for the full ten counts and you don't know if they will *ever* get up? We had both tried so hard to work through the trauma of the infidelity and repair our marriage but after a few months, it became clear he wasn't coming back. He had gone too far and was in love with someone else.

I remember I was sitting in my car the day my husband told me the second and final time he was leaving for the other woman. I raged. I pounded on the steering wheel, yelled, and frantically swung my arms. Blasting the horn, I couldn't hear anything but my heart pounding in my chest. If he just left, it would be easier, I thought. Easier than him leaving for another woman. Easier than accepting that he was in love with someone else. But all scenarios were him leaving, so no sense in rationalizing. The pain would be the same. He would be gone. He was standing there outside the passenger window. I told him I hated him and drove away. Well, I actually said I F****** hated him. I was wrapped in thick thorns of pain. I couldn't breathe. I couldn't think. I wanted to escape, but the pain just followed me as I drove.

That day one of my therapists sent me this quote by Mark Wolynn: "The stuff we think we can't handle. The conflicts and frustrations that push our edges, often push us into unfamiliar territory where we feel overwhelmed, confused, and angry. Out of these feelings, we may feel forced to take an action and this can lead us to a new understanding. One we couldn't have had otherwise. In that sense, the conflict is the driving force that leads us to experience a greater connection with ourselves."

I didn't understand. I don't want this, I thought. I didn't do anything wrong. Why is this happening to me? I just wanted him to stop. I wanted him to change. I didn't want him pushing on my edges. I didn't want things he said or did to bother me any longer. I was stuck in resistance. It felt like treading water in sand. The definition of resistance is the refusal to accept something new or different. The interesting thing is another definition for resistance is the opposite—the ability to prevent something from having an effect. We think that others are creating resistance. But really it is us.

What if we could utilize resistance to our advantage? What if we could use resistance to prevent something from having an effect on us? What if we could do a 180? What if we could go from having a refusal to accept something, to the ability to prevent that actual issue from affecting us? Do you know what? The good news is we can! At the time, though, a 180 felt impossible for me. How could I get all the way over there? Well, I didn't have to do it alone, because do you know who is good at 180s? God. Not in a cool skateboarder way, but in a way equally as extraordinary.

The conflict I had been in for the past year was driving me to experience a greater connection with myself. And this connection with myself was driving a greater connection to God. The more connected I felt to myself, the more connected I felt to God. I started to hear Him speak to me in words on a page, from the voice of a mentor or pastor, worship songs, and in quiet moments in prayer or meditation.

A year from D-day I ran the triathlon. It was a week after the car rage incident. I almost bailed, I didn't feel like doing it at all anymore. I had tried so hard to outrun the affair, but even with all my strength I couldn't win that battle. I felt defeated, tired, and unmotivated. But with some convincing from my parents, I decided to give it a go. I thought to myself, this past year would not be wasted.

I set no expectations for myself, I just wanted to finish. Let me tell you, I felt like a kid. It was one of the most exhilarating experiences of my life. Don't get me wrong. There were moments when I felt like quitting or that my legs might stop working, but so many more moments of joy, strength, excitement, and happiness.

First came the swim. I was nervous, this was my weakest portion. I jumped in, put my face in the water and pushed off. I heard the voice of my conditioning swim coach as I went from one side of the pool to the other. I focused on my breath and pacing. I remember the waves that were created in the pool from lanes over, containing many other swimmers. They were creating more resistance. Resistance I wasn't used to. I thought of when I was in the water while in labor with my first daughter, how painful but also how soothing it was. How pain is temporary. That too shall pass. Finally, my spotter raised the board signaling my last length. Thank God. Out of breath, I got out of the pool and made my way to the bikes.

The bike leg. Oh, the bike leg. It was my favorite part. I had borrowed a friend's racing bike; her name was Goldie

PART FIVE: MY TRIATHLON YEAR AND OTHER CLICHÉS

Locks. Not my friend, the bike! Yes, the bike had a name. Light as a feather, golden as the sun. She was a beauty. And a fast one at that. Out on an open highway road, I was soaring like a bird. I would look down at my watch and be clocking 45 mph at some points. I have never ridden this fast, I thought. I could have kept going further than the 15 km required. So much so that after the race my dad said, "What did you think of that hill?"

"What hill?" I asked, and we laughed.

I saw so many butterflies on my cycling leg of the race. It was incredible. I couldn't wipe the smile from my face. The gratitude I felt for my legs to be able to get me from point A to B. The smell of the fresh air. I was enveloped in the present moment. I thought, Why haven't I done this before? I love this! I think fear has always held me back from trying new things. Or going too fast. I was always cautious and thinking of the worst-case scenario. I was missing out on the beauty of being in the present moment and the exhilaration of experiencing new things. This ride changed things for me. I felt unstoppable.

Well, unstoppable until I had to get off my bike and start running. I walked a few steps and I nearly fell flat on my face on the pavement. My legs were so heavy. They felt like bricks were attached to my runners. I know why they call those training days "bricks" when you cycle then immediately run afterwards. There is nothing better to describe it. I had worked hard over the past year to remove so many bricks that were tied to me. Heavy bricks like shame, disappointment, anger, hurt, and not being enough. I was done with emotional bricks. With painful and destructive bricks. I was done with the weight and control these feelings had on me over the course of my life. It was time to untie the strings and let those bricks go.

I grabbed a cup of water, took a few more steps, and threw my cup, and my bricks in the garbage. I thought I just needed to start running. Even though I felt like I couldn't, I had to just start. My legs would follow my mind, I just needed to start moving. So, I started running. I told myself, Go slow and keep moving. You can do it. Just don't stop. I knew that if I stopped and started walking, I wouldn't start running again. The run was the hardest part of the race. I don't know if it was because it was at the end or because of how heavy my legs still felt, but it sucked. I really had to push myself at this stage. I kept my slower but steady pace and told myself to enjoy my surroundings. The day was starting to heat up. The sun was coming out and I could focus on the warm air on my skin. On my face. It felt good.

Thoughts would pop into my head about how far I had come in just one year, how many miracles happened for me. I felt grateful for all the people that came into my life that year to help me through. I thought of my therapists, how I was thankful for them. That they were true angels. And then all of a sudden, I saw the finish line ahead. I could hear music playing and people cheering for the stream of people crossing over. I had done it, I thought. I made it to the end. I accomplished what I wanted to do, just finish.

As I came across the finish line, I was looking for my parents and daughters, but they weren't there. As it turned

PART FIVE: MY TRIATHLON YEAR AND OTHER CLICHÉS

out, I far exceeded everyone's expectations. I finished at a pretty good time. They weren't there yet because they weren't expecting me to finish that quickly. I just started laughing. As I stood there trying to catch my breath, there was no disappointment that surfaced. Even though I had no one to witness my accomplishment, I felt no disappointment. Just overwhelming joy. I experienced a moment of transcendence. All the growth over the past year had accumulated into this one moment of pure joy. The social media detox had taught me to stop judging myself by others and to let go of external validation.

The triathlon taught me to take responsibility for my life and to trust myself again. I was my own witness, and that was all that mattered. I was doing this for myself, so it made perfect sense that it was just me when I crossed that finish line. I crossed a finish line that day, but for me it was really another starting line. What I thought was an end was just a beginning. The end of my marriage. The end of a future of raising our children together. The end of being a wife. The end of who I thought I was. I was starting out in new territory, somewhere I hadn't been before. And it was exciting. Scary yes, but exciting. I could be anything. I could do anything. Anything was possible now. This was not the end.

Remember D-day, June 5, 2018? Well, that day, June 5th, will now hold the honor of the day I ran a triathlon. Discovery day had been transformed into Delivery day. I was free. Free of expectations. Free from who others thought I should be. Free from judgment. Free to be me.

My identity had been so closely tied to being a certain

way. Tied to being a wife and a mother. I had forgotten who I really was. This rebirth shattered those old beliefs and like a butterfly emerging from a cocoon, I was becoming new. I didn't have a clue about what lay ahead but I learned to take it one stroke at a time. One step at a time. One day at a time. I didn't need to know the future to be ok. I would be taken care of. I would have all my needs met. Each day I would be given what I needed.

As a Catholic I grew up saying the Lord's Prayer. I had it memorized, but I never really understood the idea of "Give us this day our daily bread." That everything would be provided to you each day. There was no need for anxiety or worry. It is so hard to give up control. To surrender. We think we have to work hard for something to happen or on the flip side, worry so much for something *not* to happen. But I believe God works in the middle, where there is no worrying or striving. There is just God. And with God anything is possible. When you align yourself to this place, miracles happen. You are aligned in a place of being, more than a place of doing. You are aligned with an unlimited capacity. With a universal intelligence. It is a spiritual connection and is more powerful than any education, or designation. And it is available to everyone.

Matthew 7:7   *Ask and it will be given to you; seek and you will find; knock and the door will be opened to you.*

PART FIVE: MY TRIATHLON YEAR AND OTHER CLICHÉS

Over the past year, both my faith and endurance had a chance to grow physically and mentally.

It reminds me of Paul. Each time he faced a hardship or trial in the Bible he said, "Where I am weak, you are strong."

---

2 Corinthians 12:9 — *But he said to me, "My grace is sufficient for you, for my power is made perfect in weakness." Therefore I will boast all the more gladly about my weaknesses, so that Christ's power may rest on me.*

I started off weak and I grew stronger. I started off not being able to swim one length, to swimming 500 meters. I started off having never cycled before, to clocking 45 mph. I started off far away from God, growing closer to Him each day. Even when I was in the valley. Even when things weren't seemingly going my way. Even in the dark, I was developing an intimacy with God. My faith had many chances to be tested in that year, but each time I moved the needle forward a little bit. And a little bit more. And a little bit more. And all of those seemingly small moments built up collectively to this momentous, never-wavering faith. Faith like I have never experienced before. It started to spread into all areas of my life, from my career to finding a new home for my girls and me. God started to work through me.

PART SIX

Selfish Selflessness or Vice Versa

ONE OF A PAIR

I came home from the triathlon to an empty house. I was so proud of myself. I was so happy with what I accomplished. But I was also sad. I was sad to not have my husband to celebrate with. I was sad to realize I wouldn't have him by my side for my future accomplishments and milestones. I was sad that our divorce was starting to be finalized. This was one of those moments where two emotions existed simultaneously. I knew I had come far in the past year, but there was still sadness that existed. Grief is like that. Just when you think you have made it to the other side, it will pop up and surprise you at a sporting goods store.

I was at Mountain Equipment Co-op (MEC) on my lunch break one day soon after the triathlon. I was there on a mission. I needed to get a new workout bag/backpack. The only one I had was one of a pair. One of two, that my husband had got us years ago as matching bags. Well, I was no longer part of a pair, I thought, so I don't want that bag anymore. It reminded me of him, and I felt sad whenever I used it, so I declared I needed a new bag.

I walked in the store and went straight to the giant wall of bags. It was huge. There were so many bags to choose from. There were duffle bags, backpacks, shoulder bags, hiking bags, so many bags. I stood there and looked at the wall. Tears started to fill my eyes. I started to cry. None of these bags seemed right. Too big, too small, too expensive. I thought, What am I going to do? I need a new bag.

I didn't want a new bag. I wanted my old bag. My matching bag. I wanted to be one of two. A pair.

A nice young man asked if I needed any help and I declined. What I needed at the time he couldn't provide. I left the store crying and walked outside. I called my husband. I told him about my bag problem. He said I could keep the matching bag if I wanted to. He said he was sorry for all the missing. Sorry for everything.

It wasn't about the matching bag. I just wanted to hear his voice. I missed him so much. I didn't want to let go. Letting go of the bag would be letting go of him. Letting go of our marriage.

I wasn't ready to do that. I blew my nose and went back to work.

LETTING GO OF WHAT'S NOT ME

Another thing God was showing me that I needed to let go of was my children. To let go of the notion that they were mine.

PART SIX: SELFISH SELFLESSNESS OR VICE VERSA

He showed me that I could let go of fear and anxiety and entrust Him with them because he loves them more than we could ever love them. I know if you are a parent that sounds impossible. If you think about it, though, God created them so of course His love would be so extraordinary and substantial. More than we could ever sustain as a parent.

I was learning lessons of giving my daughters over to God because I wouldn't be with them 100% of the time now. It was hard to let go. I never dreamed of having a family so that one day I would end up divorced and only with my kids 50% of the time. I longed to be with my kids 100% of the time. But I knew it was for their good to be with their dad too. He was a good father, and he was their hero. I couldn't keep them from that. From his love. Selfishly, yes, I wanted to, but I knew what was of the highest good. And that was being with their dad half the time.

Another thing I needed to let go of was sharing the same last name as my daughters. This was heart wrenching for me. I was so attached to our family unit. To the way it was. To the way I thought it was supposed to be. There would be no more Christmas cards addressed with our last name. Or even just a simple thing, like registering the girls for swimming lessons. I would always write their last name. And each time I wrote it, it was a reminder that it was different from mine.

It expanded further from just the last name, into grieving the loss of family movie nights, board games, group hugs, and vacations. The list of losses seemed endless. The grief continued to hover around me. It has been said divorce is like a living loss. You grieve like there was a death. It is a type of death really, the death of a marriage. The death of a life lived and the life still to come. I think the hardest part of grieving a marriage is the loss of the future you thought you would have together. There are the big future losses like birthdays, celebrations, graduations, and weddings. And there are the small but just as meaningful losses like soccer games, farmers market outings, picnics, and meals. One of the saddest and hardest parts of our divorce for me was the loss of raising our children together. They were so young, only three years old and eleven months old. We wouldn't get to experience our second daughter's first steps together. Or her first words. These milestones would be celebrated separately. This broke my already damaged heart. It is also said that grief is just unexpressed love. I think that is true. I had a lot of unexpressed love.

The hard part about grief is that you have to move through it. There is no escaping it or avoiding it. It is through the moving that you heal. I witnessed this through my ex-husband's loss of his mom, and his unexpressed grief, shoved down, not allowed to move. If you don't allow yourself to grieve, I think you don't allow yourself to love.

The Bible says that God is close to the brokenhearted, and a comfort to those who mourn. I would repeat those verses when the grief felt too heavy.

Psalm 34:18 *The Lord is close to the brokenhearted and saves those who are crushed in spirit.*

PART SIX: SELFISH SELFLESSNESS OR VICE VERSA

Matthew 5:4   *Blessed are those who mourn, for they will be comforted.*

Next up on the list of losses: our family home. It sold in the middle of summer. It was necessary to sell our house for us to afford two separate homes now. I found packing up to move somewhat therapeutic. It was like I was packing up all these memories. It was a helpful step in letting go and moving on. I would always have those memories; they would just be stored in boxes now. And there would be new memories to make. It is kind of like Marie Condo for grief. Instead of looking at each item and asking if it brings you joy and the items that you say yes to you keep. I would look at items I was packing and think about the memories it held. If I felt it to be too sad, I would give it away. The process of packing and moving was definitely sad, but also healing. It was a needed step in releasing what was, for what was to come.

I remember going back to the house after the movers had cleared out all the furniture and boxes. I looked around the empty spaces and similar to what God was doing with my heart, I was clearing out space and making room for Him. I thanked the home for all it gave us. For all the memories and beautiful times I had there. And I said goodbye.

I had found a place to rent in a neighborhood I loved, and it was perfect for the girls and me. It was a bright home with a large backyard. The area was filled with young families, parks, a pool, and trails. I felt grateful. We quickly settled into this newfound sanctuary. It felt peaceful there. A welcome presence of calm from the past year and a half of chaos.

During this transition to single mom life, I quickly learned that in group events I did not want to sit at the single mom's table. That was full of self-loathing and ex-husband bashing. Then there was the happily married couple's table, I didn't fit into that one either. Hmm. Last, the single table, which consisted of mainly late twenty-year-olds who were in a different stage of life. I didn't seem to fit in anywhere.

Finding this social landscape quite defeating, I decided to create my own table and filled it with like-minded people. Empowered, compassionate single moms, healthy married couples, and mature, strong single women.

I also decided I no longer wanted to be referred to as a single mom. It felt so definitive. It felt like a crutch. Like, poor me. And is there even the term single dad? I think they just refer to a divorced dad as a dad, no? I thought of some options: single parent? Solo parent? Solo mom? These were terrible. I had just watched *Free Solo* so I think my mind was stuck in the solo zone. I went with the term co-parent. And besides, I wouldn't always be single, so why state in the title of my child-rearing status that I was.

Ok! So now that I had the name figured out, I was ready to take this on.

We had a child psychologist help create a schedule for co-parenting that was suitable for our kids. She helped us navigate this transition and supported us in this new space of having two homes for the girls. She gave recommendations, books to read, and helped to diffuse the situation when things got heated between my ex-husband and me. She even helped us write the parenting portion of our separation agreement. We both thought it would be best for my ex-husband to rent a house a few blocks away so we could make transitions between houses as easy as we could, and be close to the school the girls would attend.

Moving from being married to being co-parents is like starting a new relationship. This process was not easy. But I will share some of the things that made it easier for us. One of the things I did was change my ex-husband's name in my contact info to "The girls' dad." This was a way to release him as my former partner and start this new relationship as co-parents. When I was in communication with him via text, email, or phone, I had that distinction. From the start I made a decision to hold a vision for repair and not conflict. I decided that this co-parent relationship would be one built on kindness, peace, and cooperation. To ensure this foundation, I set an intention for a positive outcome for everyone in the future. I used each interaction as an opportunity to create a new framework built on appreciation and collaboration. And I personally committed to no longer add any further harm in the relationship.

It is a good reminder that this other person should be treated with dignity and respect, and that they are a parent to your children. That hasn't changed. You may no longer be in a relationship with them, but they are in a relationship with your child. And it is always worthwhile to treat someone how you would like to be treated.

Next, I created a competition of kindness. Acts of kindness go a long way. Once you start sending acts of kindness towards the other parent, I can assure you they will respond back with something positive your way. When you maintain putting your children first, you will always act from a place of their best interest.

For example, my ex-husband and I would often drop off milk at the other person's house when we dropped the kids off, since our youngest was still having a bottle. Another example was bringing bread from the neighborhood bakery to the other parent's house when we dropped the kids off.

These examples of milk and bread may seem small, but it is all these small things that add up, and create big waves of influence on your children. You are modeling how to treat others and especially how to treat someone that they love. Love is shown through actions. Respect is shown through actions. Your kids are always watching you and will absorb everything from you.

As I started to build this new life for the girls, I made an effort to find joy in everyday things.

From dance parties in the kitchen, to running through the sprinkler in the backyard, I set my sight on joy. I set my sight on all the good we had in our lives. Yes, bedtimes were hard. And managing working full time with caring for the girls, but we weren't alone. We had my parents who came up frequently to help us. And we had a nanny to look after the girls and the house while I went to work during the day. I built a new life, but I also built a team to support this life. Some roles were voluntary, thank you Grandma and Grandpa. But it took a team. The team made it easier to move forward. And it helped me create a balance of caring for myself

PART SIX: SELFISH SELFLESSNESS OR VICE VERSA

during this time as well as caring for my kids. Something I couldn't have done without their help. I needed the support and time to continue to heal and grow into this new life.

It was really like I was living *two* different lives. One with the girls, and one by myself. When the girls were with me, I was in full-on parenting mode. It was loud and busy and chaotic. Then when they were with their dad, I was alone. It was quiet. I had no responsibilities. I had to try to find balance in both scenarios. When I had time alone, I would focus on my personal growth, enjoying hobbies like cycling, running, doing yoga, and reading. I would spend time with friends, family, and my church community. I would volunteer and serve my community. The grief would still come and go, but each time I would move through it a little easier. A little softer. Although it felt different, I started to acclimatize to my new living arrangement. I started to feel comfortable alone and enjoyed doing things by myself. I loved my home and the space I created. It felt safe.

And I started to feel safe on my own. I no longer needed my ex-husband to fill that space. I was filling it for myself.

It was a late summer evening when I was driving home from a meditation night at a friend's home. I was coming up a hill that was lined with tall grass. To the right I saw a deer poke her head out of the grass. I slowed down to a stop. I locked eyes with the deer. I said, It's ok, don't be afraid, you can cross. It is safe. She popped back into the grass. A few seconds later she came out with her two babies. Tears filled my eyes. I continued to reassure her that it was ok to cross over. As I had that conversation with the mother deer, it was like I was talking to myself. Or God was talking to me. Telling myself it was ok to let go. To cross over. That I would be ok. That I didn't need to be afraid. The doe slowly guided them across the road to the other side. I started bawling. I was overwhelmed by the beauty of it all. By the presence of God. It was such a supernatural moment, I will always remember it.

What if one of the greatest love stories you will ever have is how you let go of someone you love? There is a great type of love that is born in that situation. A divine type of love.

What if we believed that love never dies, it is only transformed? How different would our world be? How many more relationships and marriages would end peacefully and lovingly? How many families would have restoration instead of disconnection?

What if we were taught that we can still love someone after a relationship ends? That we don't need to hate someone to get over them. That there is another way.

ANYONE BUT HER

I found myself still stuck in an unwanted triangle. My ex-husband was still with his affair partner. By this time, I had thought their fiery tryst would have burnt out, but it was still burning strong. I had the mentality that I could get over the affair and divorce, but I just didn't want them to be together any longer. I could get past the betrayal and heartbreak, but

PART SIX: SELFISH SELFLESSNESS OR VICE VERSA

if he could just choose to be with anyone else, I would be ok. Anyone but her.

I was talking to Pastor Jen about how I felt. I was crying and saying I just wanted it to be anyone but her. Repeating it over and over between sobs. I said, I will carry this hurt forever if he is with her. The pain was still raw.

I had the mentality that if they were still together it was like the affair was continuing, which brought with it all the pain I had gone through. How could I accept this woman as a step-parent to my daughters? What kind of example would that set for them? What kind of values would I be teaching them? I wanted my kids to know that the affair was wrong.

I didn't want to be haunted daily by the betrayal. And if the other woman became a step-parent, I would have the constant reminder of just that. Of the betrayal, the hurt, the pain. It was too much for me to bear.

I didn't want to forgive her. How could I forgive her? It is easier to forgive someone you love, like my ex-husband, but how do you forgive someone you don't know? Someone that caused you so much pain.

But I also knew this pain and unforgiveness would destroy me and rob me from a joyful life. I didn't know what to do, so I started praying about it. I prayed for forgiveness towards her. Even though I didn't feel like it at the time, I said the words. Even though I felt like I couldn't do it, I asked for it for her.

I think Jesus' Sermon on the Mount shines a bit of light on the subject.

Matthew 5: 43-45	*You have heard that it was said, "Love your neighbor and hate your enemy." But I tell you, love your enemies and pray for those who persecute you, that you may be children of your Father in heaven. He causes his sun to rise on the evil and the good, and sends rain on the righteous and the unrighteous.*

Every night I would pray for her. Every day my heart would transform a little bit at a time.

I was sitting in my yard in the sun one day, and God just started speaking to me. He said, "Let go of the old and let the new emerge. You have so much beauty inside of you that is trying to get out. You are so loved." I think God was telling me I had to continue to let go of who I was to become who I was meant to be.

THE EDGE OF CHAOS

At the same time, I started to think about this "becoming a new person thing" and how I was going to do that. I was working on a project for my job at the time that involved researching physics and complex systems. I had a realization that I finally needed to let go of control to evolve.

Let me explain because I know this sounds like we are going to take a turn down boring lane, but it will all make sense soon.

PART SIX: SELFISH SELFLESSNESS OR VICE VERSA

Ok, let's all put on our grade 11 school hats and get into some super-exciting stuff here.

When you look at chaos theory in physics, it is the same equation as Hakuin's "Is that so?" Remember the Zen philosopher from Part One?

Chaos theory states that in the apparent randomness of chaotic complex systems, there are underlying patterns, interconnectedness, fractals, feedback loops, and self-organization that can be broken down to a very simple level. Human life is a chaotic system. The entire Universe is made out of chaotic systems.

I started to think, Wow, we are always living at the Edge of Chaos. In a space between order and disorder. This transition space is a region of bounded instability that gives rise to a constant dynamic interplay between order and disorder. We are in a constant ping-pong game of back and forth between the two edges, not too far in one way or the other. I think this is how we evolve, and it is necessary in evolution.

What a way to think about it. Life is birthed in chaos. What a miracle.

Let me just share some physics for you quickly, stay with me here. The phrase "edge of chaos" was coined in the late 1980s by chaos theory physicist Norman Packard.[1] In science, the phrase has come to refer to a metaphor that some physical, biological, economic, and social systems operate in a region between order and either complete randomness or chaos, where the complexity is maximal.[2,3] And then in mathematics Stuart Kauffman has studied mathematical models of evolving systems in which the rate of evolution is maximized near the edge of chaos.[4]

Ok, so what they are saying is that in evolving systems shown in science and math, the rate of evolution is highest near the edge of chaos. Then can this be true in humans, animals, and the plant world? When we look at adaptation, it plays a vital role for all living organisms and systems. All of them are constantly changing their inner properties to better fit in the current environment.[5]

The most important tools for the transformation are the self-adjusting parameters essential for many natural systems. There is a phenomenon that happens in a system with self-adjusting parameters. It's called "adaptation to the edge of chaos," where there is an ability to avoid chaos.

Adaptation to the edge of chaos refers to the idea that many complex adaptive systems seem to intuitively evolve toward a structure near the boundary between chaos and order.[6] Again, this continuous ping-pong game. It feels to me like a bit of a tightrope walk between homeostasis and adaptation, as we oscillate between both.

But what stands out for me is that it *intuitively* happens. It is so interesting to me. It's like a built-in feedback loop in our mind. The underlying fabric of a chaotic system is actually order. I don't want to step on any toes here, but I think they should rename their theory from Chaos theory to Divine order theory.

I think no one likes to live in the space between order and chaos, but I do believe it is the path to equanimity. And we have more influence than we think. Remember about our state being either beautiful and harmonious, or suffering?

The state affects the ability of self-organization to happen. The state affects what we create in the world.

When you dig closer to what appears as chaos, you can find so much beauty. Have you ever looked closely at a fern? A fern is an example of a fractal, formed in a chaotic system. It has various extremely irregular curves or shapes for which any suitably chosen part is similar in shape to a given larger or smaller part when magnified or reduced to the same size. It is a picture that tells a story of the process that created it. It is infinite intelligence. And this state is inside of all of us.

I was starting to realize that I was being forced to adapt. I had to evolve or die. And not die in a literal sense but maybe in a spiritual one. Learning that I had to let go of control and to find a new perspective. A new way of being and living.

BAPTISM REDUX

I am like water.
Fluid and ever-changing.
I take shape to my surroundings.
I curve around rocks, flow over debris,
and grow stronger with force.
I act as a reflection to others,
my light illuminates to guide the way.
I flow with the current, letting love set the course.

The journey with my new church continued and I was approaching my one-year anniversary of attending, serving, and being part of this community. I felt so much love and support from the friends I made during this journey. There was a wonderful sense of a team atmosphere, it felt good to give my time each Sunday for something bigger than myself.

There was a baptism night coming up and I decided to sign up. I was baptized as an infant in the Catholic church but there was something about doing it this time by my own accord. Choosing this step felt so natural and logical to me. It is hard to describe, but it was as though my soul was longing for it, for my truest self to emerge.

It is said that baptism is an outward expression of what is happening internally. I felt that to be true for me. My internal world had changed so much over the past year and a half since D-day. God was changing me from the inside out. Getting rid of what wasn't needed any longer and forging what was. And the thought of emerging in water felt so refreshing after having gone through the fire. I felt the calling and just dove in, pun intended. I really felt the desire to declare what God was doing in my life.

I remember arriving at church and seeing this big aluminum tub set up at the front of the auditorium. I had witnessed many baptisms in the Catholic church every year while growing up. But this was nothing like I saw before. A Catholic baptism usually involves a mother or father holding a crying baby in an oversized white gown and three scoops of water being poured over its head as the priest says, "I baptize you in the name of the Father, Son and Holy Spirit."

PART SIX: SELFISH SELFLESSNESS OR VICE VERSA

This, at my new church, was a full-body dip.

I was a good mix of being excited but nervous. It was finally my turn to take the plunge. (You are welcome.) It was Pastor Jen who baptized me that night, which made it extra special for me. She was the first person I met when I had joined this church a year earlier. I got in the tub. It was surprisingly warm. There was music playing behind me from the worship team. The song playing at the time was "Reckless Love" by Cory Asbury.

The lyrics are impactful and synchronistic of this monumental event.

> *Before I spoke a word, You were singing over me*
> *You have been so, so good to me*
> *Before I took a breath, You breathed Your life in me*

I am getting emotional just writing these words now. It is truly remarkable that God will fight for us, no matter what. Even when we deny him or ignore him. Even when we turn our backs on him. I was far from God before D-day. I had turned my back on him many times. But I have learned that He is never far when we decide to come close. He is always there with his arms open. He will never leave us.

As I went under the water and came up, it felt like slow motion. I emerged and I heard everyone cheering. I smiled the biggest smile imaginable. What everyone saw on my face was pure joy. I felt pure joy. Pure joy in the face of disappointment. Pure joy in the face of infidelity. Pure joy in the face of divorce.

Hello, James. I see you. You can quit yelling at me now. I see you.

In case you skipped Part Five, which I hope you didn't, because this story is told in chronological order, I am referring to a passage from the book of James in the Bible. Here it is again for a little reminder.

James 1: 2-4
Consider it pure joy, my brothers and sisters, whenever you face trials of many kinds, because you know that the testing of your faith produces perseverance. Let perseverance finish its work so that you may be mature and complete, not lacking anything.

PART SEVEN

Totally Worth It. I Think

REPLACED

The time came for my ex-husband's partner to meet the girls. I don't think I was ever going to be ready for this moment. But it was inevitable. Best to rip the Band-Aid off quickly. I had come to a place of acceptance towards their relationship and her becoming a step-parent, but I still had this twinge in my heart. It felt familiar. Similar to being left out or replaced. Oh right, this feels familiar because I experienced it in childhood.

I felt replaced as a mother. I felt as if I wasn't needed any longer. It felt like someone else was living the life I was supposed to be in. Like I was watching from the sidelines. Wasn't this supposed to be my life? My family?

It's funny, the phrase, "supposed to be." Why do we think things are supposed to be a certain way? Like one way is wrong and one way is right. That something is good versus bad. Perhaps a perspective like the Zen Master Hakuin in Part One would serve us better. The more I think about that story, the more I think that is the way I want to live. I want to live in a state of surrender, of being open to uncertainty.

Eckhart Tolle writes about this in *A New Earth*. He describes it as chaos and higher order. He goes on to say, "When you know yourself only through content, you will also think you know what is good or bad for you. You differentiate between events that are 'good for me' and those that are 'bad.' This is a fragmented perception of the wholeness of life in which everything is interconnected, in which every event has its necessary place and function within the totality. The totality, however, is more than the surface appearance of things, more than the sum total of its parts, more than whatever your life or the world contains. Behind the sometimes seemingly random or even chaotic succession of events in our lives as well as in the world lies concealed the unfolding of a higher order and purpose."

When he is talking about knowing yourself as content, he says, "Whatever you perceive, experience, do, think or feel is content. When you think or say, 'my life,' you are not referring to the life you *are* but the life you *have* or seem to have."

That line about "the life you are" really resonated with me. What I think he is saying here is *the life I am* is not connected to anything in the physical realm. It is not connected to the content of my life, the infidelity or the divorce or my feelings. I ought not to label those things as good or bad, not even to label them at all. I am a spirit, a soul, one with God, and I can't really be touched by those events. I think to know this space beyond content is to know God.

I want to live in a space of letting go of control and just being. Trying to control everything is so exhausting. Aren't you exhausted? I am.

Eisenhower couldn't control the weather. Hakuin couldn't control anyone's actions towards him, or what was given or taken away from him. I couldn't control the outcome of my marriage, as hard as I tried. I couldn't have prevented the infidelity, just as much as I couldn't control the days my daughters were born on. (Well, I guess if you had a planned C-section you could do that one. I think you know what I mean.)

But I started to learn that I could control my perspective on any given situation.

Nothing in life is permanent. Every second, every minute, new being is birthed. I think that is what Hakuin is trying to describe in the parable. Acceptance in the challenges and in the celebrations.

Give up control. Even a little bit. Even if it feels uncomfortable. Let's do it together.

Now I know why the Serenity Prayer by the American theologian Reinhold Niebuhr is so popular and well known. It reads:

God, grant me the serenity to accept the things I cannot change, courage to change the things I can, and wisdom to know the difference.

I continued therapy and we discussed my feelings and their origins. How they were similar to the feelings I had as a child. They were one and the same. The feelings of being left out and replaced still needed to be healed and integrated. My sense of self-worth still needed some more work. A feeling that wasn't so obvious to me, or maybe more like hiding under, being left out or replaced, was jealousy. Oh, that one is a doozy. Jealousy.

I felt so jealous. I felt jealous that I wasn't included. I felt jealous when I heard of their adventures together and saw the photos. I wanted those adventures. I wanted to be in those photos. I felt a sense of lack. I wanted those family moments. I started to think, "Where do I fit into all of this? Where do I belong?"

When I dug deeper, I started to realize it all came down to how I felt about myself. It wasn't about them, it was about me. I didn't feel I was worthy enough to have those things. I didn't feel worthy of love and belonging. And those feelings started a long time ago, when I was a child. These feelings of unworthiness weren't always apparent to me as I grew into adulthood but now, looking back, I could see how they influenced the choices I made.

And then there was envy. Equally as lethal. Envy is wanting what someone else has or a fancier word would be "coveting" what someone has. The root of envy is resentment and even further I would say envy is a distrust in God. I say this because envy represents scarcity, a limited availability and of short supply. So, if you feel envious, your faith in what God has in store for you would be low, thereby showing a low sense of trust.

The Bible presents this idea as well.

---

2 Corinthians 9:8: *"And God will generously provide all you need. Then you will always have everything you need, and plenty left over to share with others."* NLT

Romans 12:14: *"Bless those who persecute you. Don't curse them; pray that God will bless them."*

I started to pray for blessings for my ex-husband and his partner. I would pray for their health and wellbeing and for an overflow of abundance in their lives.

Once I worked through and integrated these feelings, my self-worth continued to grow and I no longer felt threatened. My motherhood no longer felt threatened. My sense of self no longer felt threatened. The more worthy I felt, the more loving and accepting I felt towards her, their relationship, and her as a step-parent.

Mark Wolynn's quote sums all this learning up perfectly: "The conflict is the driving force that leads us to a greater connection to ourselves."

The challenge and conflict I was facing at that time wasn't from infidelity, or the divorce, or co-parenting. The challenge I was really facing resided within me. Understanding that was a gift, which allowed a transformation from self-betrayal to self-empowerment. A transformation of self-worth.

Let me say it again: the conflict is never outside of you. Although it may seem external, the conflict is always internal. It is a gift to come to this realization. And a gift that keeps on giving because I found it applies in all areas of life. As a parent, in work life, in friendships, even with strangers. Your neighbor is not your enemy; you are your enemy.

When your child is acting out, it's not about them, it's about you. What it is bringing up inside of you, how you respond, reflects what is going on inside of you. When your co-worker or boss says something that hits you the wrong way, it's not about them, it's about you. When a stranger says something or behaves in a way you don't find acceptable, it's not about them, it's about you.

Through all these lessons, you actually heal from infidelity by healing your self-betrayal.

Ok, let's get down to brass tacks here. The path to healing self-betrayal can be summarized in these three steps:

1) Surrender to your feelings.
2) Cultivate your own worth.
3) Step out of victimhood.

1. Surrender to your feelings.
- Surrender in the sense of letting go of control. Allow yourself to feel.
- This first step is hard. It is hard because it involves feeling hard feelings. Feelings like shame, sadness, grief, and

jealousy. We weren't always taught how to do this, so take it easy on yourself.
- Develop a practice of self-compassion and self-forgiveness. This involves accepting your own internal experience, your thoughts, and feelings. Seeing them as just that and not who you are.
- Learn to emotionally regulate. This calms your nervous system down and moves you from a sympathetic state to a parasympathetic state (from dysregulated, threat, fight and flight to calm, regulated and at rest).
- Some tools to help with this step include self-soothing behaviors like breath work, meditation, and moving emotional energy through physical activity, dance, or even screaming into a pillow.

Meditation has many benefits for your health and well-being. It creates a deep sense of connection to yourself and your divine nature and to God. It helps with emotional regulation of your nervous system. Other benefits include a reduction of anxiety and depression, a boost in the immune system via stress reduction, and enhanced self-esteem and self-acceptance. [1,2]

There are many different types of meditation. Sitting in stillness and silence. Guided meditations, using apps like The Breathing Room, Headspace, Calm, or InsightTimer. What they all do is create a space for observation of thoughts or lack of thoughts. The underlying result is the realization that you are not your thoughts; you are the observer of your thoughts. They come and go, but you remain. You, your soul, or spirit is who you are. As that observer, you can watch your thoughts go by and not be attached to them or let them define you.

2. Cultivate your own worth.
- Develop self-validating behavior. Listen to how you speak to yourself. Is it kind? Is it shaming? Ask yourself how you are feeling and write down what you need. For example, you could say, "I am feeling sad/hurt right now. I will be kind and compassionate to myself today. What I need is ………………………………." You can also tell yourself kind things like, "I am proud of myself today for getting out of my comfort zone and challenging myself." Use this method when you catch yourself wanting external validation from someone. Think about what you would hope they would say to you and then say that very thing to yourself.
- Connect to your higher power/God. Ways to do this are through prayer, meditation, music (worship music), and being in nature.[2]
- Stop judging yourself and others.
- Be the parent to your inner child. Visualize talking to your little "you," holding that person in your lap. This creates compassion for yourself which builds a strong sense of security. You can even put a picture of yourself as a child on your fridge or bathroom mirror. Every time you walk by it you can say internally, "I got you."

3. Step out of victimhood.
- Stop blaming others for how you feel. Take responsibility

for yourself, hold yourself accountable, and set boundaries.
- Use the Choose Again Method when you are feeling triggered, upset, angry by something or someone. This is a great tool to start taking responsibility for how you feel.

  Step 1: I am upset.

  Step 2: This is about me. (It is never about anyone but me.)

  Step 3: Focus on the feeling. (Ask yourself, "How do I feel?")

  Step 4: Remember the feeling. (Go back to the earliest memory of feeling the same way.)

  Step 5: Establish what the judgment of myself was at that moment. (What did it say about me that that person acted or spoke in that way? What kind of person deserves to feel that way?)

  Step 6: Embrace the truth about me. (Who I am is unchanged and unchangeable. My judgment about myself was wrong.)

  I now correct that belief by saying out loud:

  Forgive me for believing that I am ……………………………….

  (Unworthy, that whatever I do will never be enough, or ………………………………………………….)

  Forgive me for forgetting that I am ……………………………….

  (Love, peace, whole, complete)

- Realize that emotions arise from your beliefs and thoughts you have about yourself and what you believe to be true. Through practice and repetition of empowering behavior, the brain changes and new thoughts emerge from neural growth. Example: Saying "I can handle this;

it is going to be ok." Instead of saying "I can't handle this. It's never going to be ok." Your hippocampus and amygdala, the parts of your brain used for learning, memory, and emotional regulation, develop and you start to physically shape your brain. This creates self-trust.[3, 4] Neuroscientist Dr.Caroline Leaf talks about this in her book, *Switch On Your Brain*.[5] She says, we think, feel, choose—in that order.

Trust me, committing to these steps is worth it. It is worth it to allow yourself to be happy. To love again. To trust again. To experience joy.

And if you find yourself reading this book and you haven't been through infidelity, these steps will also work for you to heal your self-betrayal tendencies. Self-betrayal is universal. It doesn't only apply to infidelity. I think we are all living lives of quiet self-betrayal.

Five months after she first met the girls, my ex-husband's partner sent me an apology email. She expressed her deepest apologies and said how sorry she was for the hurt she caused me. It was an apology that wasn't needed for my healing, but it was greatly accepted and appreciated.

This was my response;

"Thank you so much for this email. I really appreciate your apology. I want you to know I hold no negative feelings and that I forgive you both. I am thankful for your loving nature towards the girls and the love and support you provide them. They truly love you.

> Looking forward to more conversations in the future and the growth of our blended family."

Gradually we began sending emails and texts. She would share little moments she had with the girls, photos of their activities, cute moments they told her stories about me. I could see how she cared for our daughters and truly loved them. I would find out more about her, how we shared similar activities growing up. We would chat at the kid's soccer games and birthday parties, human to human. I started off unable to forgive someone I didn't know or love. But with God working through me, I ended up being able to soften my heart towards her and truly forgive her. Setting us both free. In my opinion that is a miracle.

GENERATIONS DEEP

I continued to read more from Mark Wolynn's book, *It Didn't Start With You*. I began to learn more about generational trauma, to see there may be something larger at play here.

Perhaps it started generations before me.

Wolynn teaches a process of self-discovery and healing, helping us identify the emotionally charged language of our worries and fears that link to unresolved traumas from our childhood or family history. The book shows how the traumas of our parents, grandparents, and even great-grandparents can live in our unexplained depression, anxiety, fears, phobias, obsessive thoughts, and physical symptoms—what scientists are now calling "secondary PTSD."[6]

It documents the latest epigenetic research—how traumatic memories are transmitted through chemical changes in DNA—and the latest advances in neuroscience.[6]

As I dove into his work, I uncovered how the relationship with my husband was in a sense a parallel to the relationship with my mother. I understood the loss she had when her brother died but Woylnn's work was showing me something deeper. It revealed that I had cut myself off from my mother. The trauma she experienced limited how she was able to show up for me. I had judged, blamed, rejected, and cut her off. I did this subconsciously as a child and only now as an adult was I exposed to the truth of the matter.

He showed me that only when I saw my mom in a light of compassion could I resolve the pain that was preventing me from wholly embracing my life.

As I read on, Wolynn gave almost an eerily similar example of trauma and loss in his book. Here is what he wrote. "If you reject your mother, it is likely that a traumatic event stands between you and her. Perhaps her father died when she was young, or her beloved brother was killed getting off the school bus. The shock waves from such an event would affect you, but the actual event would tie up your mother's focus and attention, no matter how great her love for you.

"As a child, you might experience her as unavailable, self-absorbed, or withholding. You might then reject her, taking her depleted flow of love personally, as if somehow, she made a choice to keep it from you. The greater truth would be that the love you longed for was not available for your mother to give. Any child born into similar circumstances would likely experience a similar type of mothering.

"And so you distanced yourself from her and blamed her for not giving you what you needed, when it was really that you felt unseen for all the love you gave, or disheartened that her love could not be returned in the same way.

"When we reject our parents, we can't see the ways in which we're similar. The behaviors become disowned in us and are often projected onto the people around us. Conversely, we can attract friends, romantic partners, or business associates who display the very behaviors we reject, allowing us myriad opportunities to recognize and heal the dynamic.

"Our bodies will feel some degree of unrest until our rejected parent is experienced inside of us in a loving way."

Holy smokes! The lightbulbs were going off all around me! "This is me," I thought.

I shared this information with my parents and started to ask more questions about their parents and my great-grandparents. The generational trauma became more and more apparent.

I found out that my mom had terrible eczema when she was a baby. So much so that the average cream would not help, and the unrelenting discomfort caused her to scratch her little body so badly that it would cause bleeding and scars. Her parents, desperately wanting to help, brought her to a hospital in a neighboring town. The doctor's advice at the time involved tying up her arms to the crib so she wouldn't scratch herself. She stayed at the hospital alone without her parents, tied up in a crib. Being only a few months old, this trauma and separation from her parents, even for a short time, would have caused an interruption in the bond with her own mother. Not only that but the underlying belief of *"something is wrong with me"* was probably a narrative she developed unconsciously. And the shame that comes with that is so negatively impactful on a person.

Wolynn goes on to say, "If you reject your mother, it could be that you experienced an interruption during the early bonding process with her. Not everyone who experiences a break in the early bond will reject his or her mother. What is more likely with an interruption during this period is that you experience some degree of anxiety when you attempt to bond with a partner in an intimate relationship.

"An interruption in the mother-child bond in earlier generations can affect your connection with your mother as well. Did your mother or grandmother experience a break in the bond with her mother? The residues from these early traumas can be experienced in later generations. Not only that, but it would also be difficult for your mother to give you what she was unable to receive from her own mother."

Wow. Everything was making so much sense to me when I read this. The cycle goes deep. It goes back to my mother's early break in bonding with her own mother. And probably even further back to my grandmother's early bond with my great-grandmother.

I learned more about my maternal great-grandfather and how he became a prisoner of war in WWI. He and his family were living in Hungary and were captured by the Russian forces and held in a camp in Belarus for three years. He was released and soon after he and my great-grandmother immigrated to Canada.

So much trauma, and that is only my mother's side.

On my father's side I learned that his father, living in Croatia at the time, was drafted for WWII. Though my father doesn't think his father ended up fighting in the war, he was away training and preparing for live combat. He and my grandmother immigrated from Croatia to Canada in 1938, along with many others trying to escape the impending WWII.

My dad shared with me that his father was an alcoholic and wasn't much of a father at all. He wasn't kind or caring. Luckily, my dad had older brothers that became more of a parental figure. His father died at a young age of sixty-five. I never met my grandfather from that side. Even though he may not have faced live combat, he had to have endured some trauma from being only seventeen years old, being sent away, leaving his wife and kids, not knowing if he would return.

What did he see? What did he have to endure while there?

My eyes were opened so much by reading Wolynn's work. As I was doing this healing work around infidelity and divorce, I was actually healing the relationship with my parents, primarily with my mother. In doing so I was breaking the cycle of generational trauma for my own daughters. Perhaps now they will have to do less healing when they grow up. Perhaps in some respect I have broken the cycle for them to live more freely. To love more freely.

All the learning, unlearning, growing and healing has been worth it. Worth it for myself, for my daughters. And the effect of healing my own trauma has rippled out so far beyond my own family, reaching so many. I am grateful. My hope is for us all to heal the generational trauma that exists and to create more compassionate and loving relationships.

A year and a half had gone by and I had done a lot of therapy, reading, and learning. I felt proud of myself for how far I had come in such a short time. But there was still unrest lingering inside of me. I was still feeling a sense of strong self-hatred. How could that be? I had healed the relationship with my mother. What *else* could be left to uncover? Come on, can't a girl catch a break here?

PART EIGHT

The Scientific Art of Healing

THE ORIGINAL BETRAYAL

It was early 2020 and I would still have the recurring thought, I hate my life. I didn't know if it was discontentment from the struggles of parenting at the time or from co-parenting. I didn't know if it was associated with my job or still some feeling of grief from the divorce. But it was there lingering.

While at a weekend meditation course, I asked God to show me the root of my self-hatred. And a person appeared. This person was a friend, someone I had only fond memories of as a child. I thought that was weird. Why is this person showing up? But I was left feeling disturbed.

Serendipitously I had a therapy appointment already scheduled for the next day. I arrived and started to share about my disturbing finding from the previous day. I put the headphones on and closed my eyes as we started EMDR and Somatic Experiencing. I started to tell her about this person and the memories I had. He was a family friend and son of a babysitter whose place I had attended daily for childcare. I would be there during the day as a pre-schooler and then after school when I started kindergarten. I was there from the time I was about three to when I was seven years old.

He was about ten years older than me. I shared how we would play games and listen to records in his room. He would play his guitar. I went on to say how I had this special relationship with him. I didn't remember my sisters being there when we played, it was just him and I. He was my first friend really. My best friend. I trusted him and valued his friendship.

And then I had a memory come into my consciousness of being sexually abused by him. A memory I had never had before. With my eyes closed I started to feel sensations in my body. With my therapist's help I breathed through what I was feeling. It was like I was viewing the event from outside, but I also was feeling the fear inside of my body. I was trembling and crying as I spoke to my therapist. It was like I was experiencing the event for the very first time. I even said at one point, "I think I may pee my pants." She helped me release the fear as we spoke. The hour and a half went by and I opened my eyes.

I looked at her and said, "I feel so betrayed."

I had trusted this person. He was my friend. How could he have done this to me? I was confused and angry. This was all too familiar.

She went on to explain that I had disassociated from the trauma because I wasn't able to process it at the time. I was just a child. It was my brain and nervous system's way of protecting itself. The trauma became locked in my subconscious mind and stored in my body. Just like we learned from Dr. Peter Levine in Part Three.

I believe that my nervous system was finally at a place of safety that my mind and body could finally let this memory come to the surface and into my consciousness. All the prior EMDR and Somatic Experiencing we had been doing over the past two years had finally allowed my body and subconscious to release this original trauma. All of the processing of the trauma from the infidelity had led me to this very moment to heal the childhood trauma of being sexually abused.

My oldest daughter was five years old at this time, the same age as I believe I was when the abuse started. Seeing her at this age was a trigger for me. I was terrified of her being sexually abused and would be flooded with anxiety around it happening to her.

The recurring thought, I hate my life, was from long ago. Of course I had a thought that I hated my life; at the time I probably did. I hated what was happening to me and I couldn't distinguish the action from myself, so in turn the thought was created, I hate my life, or I hate myself, when really the truth was, I hated the action of abuse I was a victim of. I hated that I was stuck in a place of no escape.

Wow. Everything was making so much sense to me. I was flooded with memories of fearing being home alone as a child. Being scared of going into my basement on my own. Being scared of the dark. I had ongoing stomach aches in grade two and asked to go home almost every day. These digestive issues stayed with me well into adulthood.

I had been living in fear my whole life and I finally knew why.

It was quite disturbing to find out something of this magnitude, not having ever known it my whole life. It was bizarre. The first thought I had after this session was, I can't tell my parents. They won't believe me. I was thirty-seven years old and I still thought that. This was revealing for me. If at thirty-seven I didn't think that my own parents would believe me, I can see why at five years old I held the same belief. Plus, I was burdened with shame and guilt, taking on the responsibility of what happened.

Everything started to make so much sense. All these feelings of not being enough, being unlovable, having low self-worth, fearing abandonment, and fearing being left alone. Of course I felt that way. I went through something no child should ever go through, and it shaped how I felt about myself. It shaped my view of who I was and how I saw the world. It created anxiety and left me with a dysregulated nervous system, living in fear.

Trauma expert Dr. Gabor Maté shares in his work that trauma, from the Greek for "wound," is not what happens to you; it is what happens inside you as a result of what happens to you.

I continued to process this with my therapist for a year. We continued to do EMDR and Somatic Experiencing to help release the fear and trauma from my body.

She helped me process the betrayal and sadness around it and how it had caused me to suffer from Complex PTSD. Complex PTSD is similar to PTSD or Post-traumatic stress disorder. The difference is that PTSD usually occurs from a single traumatic event and c-PTSD is an outcome of repeatedly experienced traumatic events, such as violence, neglect, abandonment, or abuse.

Symptoms may include:[1,2]

- feelings of shame or guilt
- difficulty controlling emotions
- periods of losing attention and concentration (dissociation)
- physical symptoms, such as headaches, dizziness, chest pains, and stomach aches
- cutting off from friends and family
- relationship difficulties
- destructive or risky behavior, such as self-harm, alcohol misuse, or drug abuse
- suicidal thoughts
- self-abandonment
- toxic shame
- emotional flashbacks

One of my therapists recommended the book *Complex PTSD: From Surviving to Thriving* by Pete Walker.[3] This book is a practical guide to recovering from lingering childhood trauma. It includes many examples of his clients' journeys of healing. Traumatizing abuse can occur on verbal, emotional, spiritual, and physical levels. The book was and is to this day a very helpful tool for my own healing journey of trauma and c-PTSD.

Adults with c-PTSD may lose their trust in people and feel separated from others.[1]

In addition, if you have c-PTSD you may experience what some people call an "emotional flashback," in which you have intense feelings that you originally felt during the trauma, such as fear, shame, sadness, or despair. You might react to events in the present as if they are causing these feelings, without realizing that you are having a flashback.[2,3]

Walker describes flashbacks as amygdala hijackings, because of the unnecessary triggering of our fight/flight instincts. He shares that emotional flashbacks are sudden and often prolonged regressions to the overwhelming feeling-states of being an abused/abandoned child. And these flashbacks, unlike PTSD, do not typically include a visual component. These feelings can include overwhelming fear, shame, alienation, rage, grief, and depression.[3]

All the trauma from this original betrayal and abuse came out when I went through the trauma of infidelity two years prior. I was having the same intense feelings as an adult that I originally felt when I was a child—fear, shame, sadness, despair, anger. No wonder I felt like I was dying. These feelings held such an emotional charge. The feelings from the childhood trauma were the exact feelings I felt from infidelity. They needed to be uncovered to be healed, and the infidelity was the exact vehicle they needed to escape to the surface.

Processing the anger around this event was hard. It was hard to connect to the anger because it was something that happened so long ago. And because I didn't know about it for so long. It felt unnecessary, I guess. But my therapist knew I had to get there for this process to be fully released and healed. We finally got there, and I was able to let it out.

As the year passed, I came full circle to a place of forgiveness for him. I felt compassion for him as I learned in most cases perpetrators of abuse have been a victim of abuse themselves. Not that it makes what happened ok, but, like I mentioned earlier about forgiveness, it is the process of letting go of the pain associated with the person or event that is important. I didn't have to hold onto that pain or anger any longer. I could let it go and no longer allow it to have any hold on me.

I believe that it is important to talk about hard subjects like this. There is so much shame around it, but it is when we let our shame be shared that we can be free of the shame itself.

I started to do some research on childhood sexual abuse. The statistics I came across were alarming. Did you know 95% of child sexual abuse victims know their perpetrator, and that one in three girls and one in six boys experience an unwanted sexual act?[4] I did not know these stats. It did make me feel less alone in the process of healing though.

And it made me think of how many others may have gone through a similar experience, not even remembering the trauma itself. If one third of the female population and one sixth of the male population has experienced some form of unwanted sexual act, that is millions of people walking around with trauma. I wonder what the statistics are of individuals having no memory of it.

My hope is that my vulnerability and sharing may provide enough safety for others to heal from any childhood trauma they may have experienced. Or even investigate the root cause of their feelings around shame, unworthiness, anxiety, or depression. I wonder how many of us are walking around carrying a trauma that we dissociated from as a child. Something that was so horrific or awful that our bodies are too terrified to make it known. To allow it to be healed. My hope is that it may unlock trauma in others and give them the courage to face the fear of knowing. The fear of feeling it.

Dr. Ron Siegel says, "When we bury feelings, we bury them alive. We wind up living with a heart and mind that are filled with landmines easily triggered when we go through the world."

In this process of uncovering trauma we can gently start to disarm the landmines that live within us. Providing us with a life no longer run by fear, shame, or terror. There is another way to live, and it is available to all of us.

There are some great organizations who do incredible work if you would like to learn more or access resources. Little Warriors and Breaking Free Foundation are two. In his books and more recently in his film, *The Wisdom of Trauma*, Gabor Maté talks a great deal about trauma and its connection to addiction. They are worth reading and watching.

BECOMING A NEUROSCIENTIST

It is heartbreaking to learn the cycle of trauma and how it plays out from childhood to adulthood.

As an adult, I was going to break this cycle. I was going to become a neuroscientist! Well not really, but sort of. More like a brain surgeon, or a mind surgeon.

During the year alongside my therapy and EMDR, I dove into neuroscience. I know what you are thinking, How does a person just casually dive into neuroscience? It's far from taking up a fun hobby such as painting. Let me explain.

I attended a talk by Dr. Caroline Leaf and was left both inspired and determined to become a neuroscientist. Dr. Leaf is a communication pathologist and cognitive neuroscientist with a Masters and PhD in Communication Pathology and a BSc Logopedics, specializing in cognitive and metacognitive neuropsychology. Since the early 1980s she has researched the mind-brain connection, the nature of mental health, and the formation of memory. She was one of the first in her field to study how the brain can experience change (neuroplasticity) with directed mind input.

I ate up every word she said. She talked about the mind and brain and how they are not the same. Your mind uses your brain. Your mind is expressed through your brain and body. The mind is 99%. The body is 1%. If I could insert a brain exploding emoji here, I would. Her words were revolutionizing how I viewed my life and the world. She went on to say the consciousness of your mind is becoming the cells of the matter of your brain. (Another brain exploding emoji, please!) And she shared that the thoughts in your mind are non-physical quantum waves of energy. Don't get me started on quantum physics, or I won't shut up. To say I was fascinated is an understatement.

The funny thing was this was all making sense to me. It was so empowering. My brain was moldable like plastic, and I could change it. I could create new neural pathways and change old thoughts and beliefs. I wanted to learn it all. I bought her book, *Switch On Your Brain*, at that talk. I read it and absorbed all the information.

I started to use her NeuroCycle app. It is a five-step program that is designed to help overcome anxiety, depression, toxic thinking, and trauma. Using this program Dr. Leaf teaches you how to find the root of the toxic thought and habit that is causing mental health issues. She then helps you reconceptualize the root and rebuild a healthy new thought pattern and habit to change behavior.[5]

I would do the twenty-one-day cycles for each root thought. I made a list and crossed each one off as I did a cycle for it. These included thoughts of being unlovable, not worthy, not good enough, abandoned, and being afraid of being left alone. I also did cycles for other thoughts like, I wish things were different, and, I can't do this on my own.

I continued using this NeuroCycle app regularly for a year. I think it was an integral part in my healing and processing the trauma of sexual abuse. I had a lot of time on my hands, as it was 2020. Most of the world was shut down. I was laid off right before the pandemic hit in March of that year and I was provided the time I needed to focus on healing. I was provided time to be with my young daughters. This was a blessing of its own.

It took me a year to have the courage to share this with my parents. I didn't want to traumatize anyone, so sharing this information from a healed place made sense to me. I also didn't want them to feel like they didn't protect me or like they were bad parents.

I don't know if you could prepare someone for this type of news. My parents were just as disturbed as I was. Very shocked and very angry. We talked about it for a while and I assured them that I had done much healing around this and that I was ok. That I had been processing it for a year now with my therapist and that it wasn't controlling or damaging my life in any way. And that I had come to a place of forgiveness for him. They were glad I told them. And contrary to my deeply held fear, they believed me. Of course they did, as would I if one of my daughters told me something like this. A parent's love is like no other.

I do believe the infidelity was a Divine intervention, allowing for the underlying childhood trauma to be brought to the surface to be healed. The original betrayal could only be healed by a trauma of the same magnitude. It is similar to Newton's third law in physics, also known as the law of action and reaction. For every action (force) in nature there is an equal and opposite reaction.[6]

The self-betrayal had to be healed at the root of the self-hatred.

And that is one of the reasons I call this book *The Gift of Infidelity*. There have been many gifts along the way, but this perhaps was the greatest gift of all. Infidelity provided me with the key to the freedom to live my life as I was meant to live it. No longer bound by fear, anxiety, or shame.

God never wanted me to live that way. He wanted me to live a full life of joy, peace, and love. Free from shame, guilt, and fear.

Albert Einstein said, "There are only two ways to live your life. One is as though nothing is a miracle. The other is as though everything is a miracle." I think I would like to live like the latter.

To live as though everything is a miracle.

The process of healing from this childhood trauma is still ongoing. Healing the nervous system takes time and work. But I can say I am at a place of freedom, and that is a miracle. I consider infidelity to be a miracle, the divorce to be a miracle, and the love I still hold for my ex-husband to be a miracle.

And I think throughout these past years, I have started to become who I was meant to be.

As I let go of who I thought I was, or who I was supposed to be, my true self has emerged.

That was a miracle.

I challenge you to shift your perspective. A miracle-minded perspective.

What can be born from this situation? What is the good that can come from this challenge? How is this happening for me and not to me? How many births are not seen? How many ideas come from hard situations but are glossed over? How many successes come out of failures that we don't see? You can't see them if you are looking in the wrong direction. Which way are you looking?

What if we looked at life as a series of births? Or rebirths. And let the divine timing take its place. There is no rushing or pushing or inducing. It is just so. Like Hakuin so eloquently stated.

I have come to realize God's plan is bigger than my plans. That he is in the business of supernatural events and creations. He in the business of evolving us to be the greatest expressions of him.

We can't talk about betrayal without talking about one of the most well-known betrayals of all time. If you Google most well-known betrayers, guess whose name pops up? Judas.

I wonder if Judas had not betrayed Jesus, would God's plan have succeeded. Surely it would have. I'm sure he would have found another person to carry out the plan. I think in this story Judas represents our humanity and Christ represents God being *with us* in our humanity. There will be human things like betrayal that will happen in our lives, but God will always be there with us.

Betrayal was in his destiny for Jesus to achieve God's plan. Jesus had to die for us to live. He had to die for us to be able to be free to live with God eternally. For us, for our humanity, to be forgiven and set free of guilt, shame, and condemnation. It was a miracle. It was a love story. Full of all the emotions we as humans feel throughout the course of a lifetime. Jesus felt those. Betrayal, anger, sadness, hurt. He was mocked and ridiculed. He felt what it was like to feel hated. But he also felt what it was like to be loved. Loved by God. And love overcomes all.

My prayer for us is, May all hatred be turned to love.

And love overcame all when Jesus rose from the dead three days after this death. Love overcame all with the resurrection. Jesus shared this with his disciples shortly before his death.

| John 16:33 | *I have told you these things, so that in me you may have peace. In this world you will have trouble. But take heart! I have overcome the world.* |

I don't know if they could truly grasp the concept until after the resurrection. But Jesus was trying to prepare them for it. I think he is sharing with us all in this verse that he knows the heartache and pain we will experience in our lives, but there can be peace in the pain. There can be joy and love in the pain when we align our hearts with Him. We don't have to be in pain alone. And the pain won't always be there. Love will overcome. (This paragraph was for you, James. I think I get the point now.)

FORGIVENESS LIKE A FLOWING RIVER

It was my first time speaking at an online conference on the topic, The Gift of Infidelity. I was preparing and going over my message when I received an email from my ex-husband. He wanted to let me know that he was back together with his affair partner. I felt the tightness in my body as I read it. The familiar feeling in the pit of my stomach.

For the past two years I think I had longed for their relationship to end, so I wouldn't have the constant reminder of the affair. If he had chosen someone different, it would be easier to stomach. Easier if I didn't have to co-parent with her and accept her as a step-parent. Easier not to see them together almost every day. The tightness in my body released and I heard this voice. You could say it was God speaking to me or my highest self speaking to me and I said to myself. "Andrea, you are no better than her. Who are you to judge her?" I felt tears in my eyes and was filled with compassion. There was no resistance. This felt true. This voice was right. I am no better than her and she is no less of a person than me. We are all the same. I went on to do my talk that morning and from that day forward I have had a shift in perspective towards her.

I knew if I kept referring to her as his "affair partner," then that is what she would be to me. So that day I dropped the "affair" label and from then on, I referred to her as his "partner."

I shed another layer. A new version of myself was born. A more compassionate and accepting version.

I started to think more about forgiveness, reading many authors' takes on the definition of forgiveness. Agreeing with all of them. Mixing and matching in my mind. I thought I solved the forgiveness puzzle.

I learned that forgiveness is both a selfish and selfless act. On one side it is selfish because it is a gift you give yourself. You are releasing all the hurt and pain associated with an act, giving yourself freedom. But it is also selfless because it releases the other person from any pain, shame, or guilt, freeing them as well. It is an energy shift internally. Disentangling you from the web of another, it releases all the emotions associated with the original wrongdoing.

Maybe that is why God tells us to forgive others and *we* will be forgiven.

Luke 6:37 *Do not judge, and you will not be judged. Do not condemn, and you will not be condemned. Forgive, and you will be forgiven.*

I discovered forgiveness can't be forced. It is an outcome. Like the birth of a baby, when it is ready it will be born. It is an outcome of understanding, processing, and feeling. It is an outcome of a transformation of the heart and the mind. And I also discovered it is an ongoing process. That it is not one and done. Like the thawing river I saw from the ridge, the ice will take a while to melt.

I tried so hard to forgive. To let go. Praying about it. Writing about it. Asking for it to happen. I knew I wanted to forgive, but I just couldn't *make* it happen. No matter how hard I tried. Intellectually I understood and believed. But I didn't feel it in my body. In my heart.

Then I decided to change tactics. I said, God, I don't know how to forgive them, I need you to do this for me. I am only a human. Please take this bitterness, resentment, and unforgiveness from me. I give it all to you.

And then one day it was just there, waiting for me. Like a plastic bag blowing around in the wind. It landed on my doorstep. I opened the door and it was there. Freedom was there. Love was there. Peace was there.

It's funny. As I thought about the Prayer of St. Francis, I started to realize the very thing I wanted most I had to give to someone else.

The second half of the prayer says;

May I not so much seek
To be consoled as to console,
To be understood as to understand,
To be loved as to love,

For it is in giving that we receive,
It is in pardoning that we are pardoned,
And it is in dying that we are born to eternal life.

This was the magic equation I was looking for all along. I wanted so much to be consoled, to be understood, to be loved. But it wasn't about me. It was about what I could give to others. I learned to console, to understand, to love, and to forgive. And in the very act of doing so I received it. It is truly magical.

You know the saying, "Hell has no fury like a woman scorned." It is a proverb adapted from lines in *The Mourning Bride*, a tragic play by English playwright William Congreve, first performed in 1697. The line is said by the character Zara, a queen whose capture entangles her in a lethal love triangle.[7] The expression means that no one is as angry as a woman who has been romantically rejected or betrayed. I discovered there is a second part to this verse.

"Heaven has no fury like love turned to hatred."

The original text reads;

" Heav'n has no rage, like love to hatred turn'd, Nor hell a fury, like a woman scorn'd."

No one really talks about the second part of the verse. They just focus on the rage and scorned part. I think the more powerful version of this proverb could be;

"Heaven has no adoration like hatred turned to love. Nor hell a fury like a forgiving woman."

Hell would not exist if hatred was turned to love. It would not exist if rage and anger were transformed into forgiveness. I should be a scorned woman. I check all the boxes. Betrayed, rejected, and full of rage. But I am not. I broke the script. Well, God broke the script. He broke the script when he sent Jesus two thousand years ago and sacrificed his life for us. He showed us that even in the times humanity is at its worst, there can be forgiveness and compassion.

A powerful woman is a forgiving woman, not a scorned woman. You want to see miracles unleashed, choose forgiveness. If you want to see God move mountains in front of your eyes, choose forgiveness. Forgiveness sets you free. It also sets the other person free from their suffering. I never acted out of anger towards her this whole time. I never unleashed my anger onto her. (Much credit goes to my therapist who held me accountable for my behavior, thankfully, repeating to me, "Do not act out towards her.") I never called her a homewrecker or degraded her. I did express my rage and anger in my therapy sessions and in my journal. I used those means as a vehicle to move the emotions and feelings I had. I discovered that hurting her would not make me feel better. We may think that it will help to ease our pain by causing someone else pain, but it is quite the opposite.

My heart began to soften towards her. I could see how we were similar. I could see myself in her, we were one. And I could see that she was actually a really nice person.

I was so worried about what I would be teaching my daughters if I accepted her as a step-parent. I was worried that when my daughters grew up, they would think that what they did was ok. I wanted to teach them values and morals that were pure and full of integrity. All the while I was missing the point.

By the very act of forgiving her and accepting her into our blended family, I would be teaching my daughters the exact morals and values I wanted for them. Values like compassion, forgiveness, and love. I would be teaching them that people make mistakes, but those mistakes don't define who they are. I would be teaching them resilience, strength, and courage.

And for myself, I began to realize I could accept her without judgment and blame and release the pain she caused me. I could finally release myself from the triangle.

AN EVER AFTER LOVE

This may be one of the most unorthodox love stories ever told. Not the type of love story you are used to, I am sure. But oh, is it a powerful one. One I cannot take full credit for.

Maybe my old wedding handkerchiefs were right all along. We did live happily ever after. But not in the way *I* had planned. God had a bigger plan for our lives. A plan that would change many lives, far beyond any distance or place we could see with our own eyes.

Love. True love. Unconditional love is what we should all strive for. Love that changes beyond what we can see. Love that changes hearts. Love that expands further than the space between two people. Love that heals families. Love that forgives. Divine love. An Ever After love.

God came to earth, in human form, to show us how to love. And I don't think we have the capability to love in this unconditional way without His help. I just don't think it is humanly possible. I certainly wouldn't be here writing this today without Him.

We try so hard to love others, but we hate ourselves. And we wonder why it doesn't work.

Because to love someone else means we have to love ourselves, and we just don't know how to do that. We live in a world where it is second nature to betray ourselves. To not be who we truly are. Or love ourselves for who we truly are. Our divine selves, our child selves.

This love has to start with ourselves. Before any conditioning, or trauma, or altering of our perceptions of who we are. I think this is a life's work. A daily practice. When you come up against an external situation that is pushing on your edges, it is a moment to love yourself a little more. And when we fall, we get back up again and recommit. To love yourself truly, this, right here, is the secret sauce.

As I came to know that self-betrayal is a disconnection to self, I started to realize that self-betrayal, at its core, is actually a disconnection to God. To our soul. To the Holy Spirit.

To our true nature. There was another layer to uncover.

How much more disconnected can you be than to be disconnected to the very life source that made you? To the very source of life itself. There is an interconnectedness in everything that exists in the universe and the universe itself. We exist in the push and pull at the edge of chaos, creating, evolving, and adapting. Remember the fern from Part Six? I can see myself in the fern, having been formed in a chaotic system. I am a picture that tells the story of the process that created me.

When we try to disconnect, or when we self-betray, we create suffering. That is why I think connection is so important as humans. We need interconnectedness to survive. And when I think about religion and church, it isn't a place or a doctrine to abide by. Church exists in people. It is in the way we act, how we think, in our relationships. It is inside of us, and people are the reflection of it. They reflect the connection or disconnection. It is within others that we see God, experience His presence. I should say it is one way to experience God, but I think it is probably the most significant way, in another.

When I reflect on my Catholic upbringing, I now see that the reason I found a disconnection to God was probably because I was surrounded by a lot of disconnected people. People like me, who believed in something but didn't have a relationship with it. People who attended every Sunday, memorized prayers, followed the doctrine, but maybe like me, felt something was missing. It wasn't that I felt a disconnection to Catholicism, I felt a disconnection to God, but I didn't know that at the time.

I am so grateful for my Catholic upbringing and everything I learned from it. It laid the groundwork to get me to where I am today. But I am also grateful for the next phase of my faith that was cracked open while going through infidelity and the connection that was created to the source of the One that made me. Sometimes it takes a breakdown of reality to really see. Sometimes it takes a grenade to blow up all you have ever known, to know what is unlimited.

To know what is unlimited is to know God. From this unlimited space, anything is possible.

If I could be cracked open through pain, maybe the same kind of transformation is possible through love. That equation I haven't solved yet. Stay tuned.

Or maybe it is just like James said, that it is the *joy* in the suffering that actually transforms us. The Divine love and grace that falls upon us when we are in that trial, not the trial itself but the love that comes from God when we are in the trial creates the metamorphosis.

Eckhart Tolle says in *A New Earth*, *"The fire of suffering becomes the light of consciousness."*

And James then says at the end of the chapter, *"Let perseverance finish its work so that you may be mature and complete, not lacking anything."*

I think that is the evolution of humanity right there. To be lacking nothing.

A shift from scarcity to abundance. A shift from competition to comradery. A shift from hate to love. A shift from fear to hope.

There is no needing, or wanting, or taking from another person or thing. Or achieving or succeeding. It will not be so much about how much money can I make, but more like how much I can give away. Instead of taking from the Earth, it will be how I can give back to the planet.

Our minds and hearts are to be transformed to answer the question, How can I love? How can I serve? How can I help someone else? How can I forgive? Who can I forgive? How can I understand? How can I console? Less me, more us.

This evolution needs to be a radical shift in thinking and being. A commitment of a different way of being in the world. Going against the grain of society. All you need to do is ask. Ask for a transformation of your heart and mind. To see how God sees. Ask for Him to come into your heart.

Jesus said this:

Luke 17:20-21   *"The coming of the kingdom of God is not something that can be observed, nor will people say, 'Here it is,' or 'There it is,' because the kingdom of God is in your midst."*

And the most important footnote of this whole book is included here:

Luke 17:21   *"The kingdom of God is within you!" NLT*

Jesus explains this as well when he talks about childlike faith.

Matthew 18:3   *And he said: "Truly, I tell to you, unless you change and become like children, you will never enter the kingdom of heaven."*

I believe he is showing us how to live in the kingdom of heaven now, in the present, as children do. Showing us how to live in joy and peace with creative minds and soft hearts. We can look to the attributes of young children to see further into Jesus' message. Qualities like wonder, awe, playfulness, eternal hope, exuberance, and a willingness to learn and grow. How easily children forgive, and love. They hold no bias and naturally see the good in others. How often do we talk about the resilience of children? I think it is something that we are born with and as we grow up the weight of the world chips away at this resilience until we think we no longer possess it. But I assure you, it is still there, buried in your soul. Accessing it may be painful, but it is also beautiful and necessary.

PART EIGHT: THE SCIENTIFIC ART OF HEALING

Psychologists define resilience as the process of adapting well in the face of adversity, trauma, tragedy, threats, or significant sources of stress—such as family and relationship problems, serious health problems, or workplace and financial stressors. As much as resilience involves "bouncing back" from these difficult experiences, it can also involve profound personal growth.[8]

That is the key: profound personal growth. That is what I discovered and unlocked within myself.

The cool kids call it PPG. Might even make a rap about it.

MY PRAYER FOR YOU

May you receive the everlasting love that is available for you.
May you know the true nature of who you are.
May you give what you want to receive.
May you experience peace in your mind and heart.
May you be unlimited.
May your self-hatred be transformed to self-love.
May you be flowing water.
May you give and receive Ever After love.
May you experience miracles.
May you know God.

ACKNOWLEDGEMENTS

I feel so much love and gratitude to God that I was able to write this book as it was the most joyful experience I have ever had. I always say this book wasn't written by me, but through me.

To my ex-husband, thank you for providing me the opportunity to love you. To love you when it wasn't easy, when it was messy, and when it seemed impossible. For in loving you I found out how to love myself.

To my mom and dad, thank you for all the love and support you provided (and continue to provide) for the girls and me.

To my daughters, thank you for showing me who I really am. For reflecting the beauty, strength, and resilience within me.

To the girls' step-mom, thank you for being an amazing co-parent. You are truly a beautiful addition to our blended family.

Kathleen, Sharon, and Dr. Hagan, thank you for joining me on my rollercoaster. You are angels sent from heaven and have changed my life. I know you would all say something in your therapist voice like, No, Andrea, you changed your life. But truly I couldn't have done it without you.

To Jen, thank you for dragging me to the pool week after week. I love you.

To my sisters, Janine, and Kristin, for always being supportive and loving.

To Pastor Jen, thank you for walking with me in the darkest days.

To Nancy Henderson, thank you for waking me up at 5am everyday for a month straight, to practice meditation with you. It truly changed my life.

To Dr. Johal, thank you for being a source of healing, a mentor, and cheerleader. My nervous system thanks you.

To Mick Silva, my editor, thank you for your expertise and guidance on this project. You really brought this book to the next level.

To Trevor McMonagle, my proofreader, for your extraordinary attention to detail and way with words. Thank you for elevating this story beyond what I thought was possible.

To Marc Stoiber, my speaking coach, thank you for helping me shape this book before it came into written form.

To Keren, thank you for believing in me before anyone else hopped on for this ride. And for being the catalyst for me to write this book.

And to all my friends and family, old and new, I am thankful for your love and support.

With much gratitude and love, I thank you all.

CRITICAL SOURCES

PART ONE: She Never Sees It Coming
Sources:

1. https://www.history.com/topics/world-war-ii/d-day

PART TWO: All His Fault. For Sure
Sources:

1. https://www.britannica.com/science/hippocampus

The hippocampus, which is located in the inner (medial) region of the temporal lobe, forms part of the limbic system, which is particularly important in regulating emotional responses.

2. https://www.ncbi.nlm.nih.gov/pmc/articles/PMC3004979/

3. https://www.britannica.com/science/amygdala

4. https://www.tandfonline.com/doi/full/10.1080/17470919.2017.1311939

5. https://www.attachmentproject.com/blog/avoidant-attachment-style/

PART THREE: My Brutiful Frenemy Self-Betrayal
Sources:

1. Maria Marshall; Edward Marshall (2012). *Logotherapy Revisited: Review of the Tenets of Viktor E. Frankl's Logotherapy.* Ottawa: Ottawa Institute of Logotherapy. ISBN 978-1-4781-9377-7. OCLC 1100192135. Retrieved 16 February 2020.

2. Frankl, Viktor (1 June 2006). *Man's Search for Meaning.* Beacon Press. ISBN 978-0-8070-1427-1. Retrieved 8 May 2012.

3. Frankl, Viktor (1 September 1988). *The Will to Meaning: Foundations and Applications of Logotherapy.* Meridian. ISBN 978-0-452-01034-5. Retrieved 17 May 2012.

4. https://journals.sagepub.com/doi/abs/10.1177/0146167217695558

https://www.psychologytoday.com/us/blog/between-cultures/201805/in-helping-others-you-help-yourself

5. Feske, Ulrike (June 1998). "Eye Movement Desensitization and Reprocessing Treatment for Posttraumatic Stress Disorder". Clinical Psychology: Science and Practice. 5 (2): 171–181. doi:10.1111/j.1468-2850.1998.tb00142.x.

6. https://www.psycom.net/emdr-therapy-anxiety-panic-ptsd-trauma/

7. https://traumahealing.org/se-101/

8. https://www.mindbodygreen.com/0-13730/5-things-everyone-should-know-about-acceptance.html

PART FOUR: Doping Out on Facebook
Sources:

1. http://repositorio.ispa.pt/bitstream/10400.12/3364/1/IJSP_998-1009.pdf

2. https://www.insightforliving.ca/read/insights-bible/ruth?gclid=CjwKCAjw6dmSBhBkEiwA_W-EoF4Ts7jFt87A_R_YOuvki1K8rdxpO0wnxn1TO21PyGOZfCb-YibUbxoCpz0QAvD_BwE

PART SIX: Selfish Selflessness or Vice Versa
Sources:

1. H. Packard, Norman (1988). "Adaptation Toward the Edge of Chaos". University of Illinois at Urbana-Champaign, Center for Complex Systems Research. Retrieved 12 November 2020.

2. Shulman, Helene (1997). *Living at the Edge of Chaos, Complex Systems in Culture and Psyche*. Daimon. p. 115. ISBN 9783856305611. Retrieved 11 November 2020.

3. *Complexity Thinking in Physical Education : Reframing Curriculum, Pedagogy, and Research; edited by Alan Ovens, Joy Butler, Tim Hopper*. Routledge. 2013. p. 212. ISBN 9780415507219. Retrieved 11 November 2020.

4. Gros, Claudius (2008). *Complex and Adaptive Dynamical Systems A Primer*. Springer Berlin Heidelberg. p. 97, 98. ISBN 9783540718741. Retrieved 11 November 2020.

5. Strogatz, Steven (1994). *Nonlinear dynamics and Chaos*. Westview Press.

6. Kauffman, S.A. (1993). *The Origins of Order Self-Organization and Selection in Evolution.* New York: Oxford University Press. ISBN 9780195079517.

PART SEVEN: Totally Worth It. I Think
Sources:

1. https://www.ncbi.nlm.nih.gov/books/NBK279390/

2. https://news.harvard.edu/gazette/story/2018/04/harvard-researchers-study-how-mindfulness-may-change-the-brain-in-depressed-patients/

3. https://www.ncbi.nlm.nih.gov/pmc/articles/PMC6660260/

4. https://www.nature.com/articles/npp2009121

5. https://drleaf.com/collections/books/products/switch-on-your-brain

6. https://markwolynn.com/it-didnt-start-with-you/

PART EIGHT: The Scientific Art of Healing
Sources:
1. https://www.nhs.uk/mental-health/conditions/post-traumatic-stress-disorder-ptsd/complex/#:~:text=Complex%20PTSD%20may%20be%20diagnosed,the%20trauma%20for%20a%20long

2. https://www.mind.org.uk/information-support/types-of-mental-health-problems/post-traumatic-stress-disorder-ptsd-and-complex-ptsd/complex-ptsd/

3. Complex PTSD:From Surviving to Thriving by Pete Walker

4. Source: Child Sexual Abuse (The Canadian Badgley Royal Commission, Report on Sexual Offences Against Children and Youths), 1984. (pg. 175) (pg. 215-218)

5. https://drleaf.com/pages/current-clinical-trials

6. https://www1.grc.nasa.gov/beginners-guide-to-aeronautics/newtons-laws-of-motion/

7. Congreve, W., *The Works of Mr. Congreve: Volume 2. Containing: The Mourning Bride; The Way of the World; The Judgment of Paris; Semele; and Poems on Several Occasions*, Adamant Media (2001), facsimile reprint of a 1788 edition published in London.

8. https://www.apa.org/topics/resilience

RESOURCES MENTIONED

The Bible, NIV & NLT when noted

Complex PTSD: From Surviving to Thriving: A Guide and Map for Recovering from Childhood Trauma, Pete Walker

The Four Sacred Secrets: For Love and Prosperity, A Guide to Living in a Beautiful State, Preethaji and Krishnaji

Getting the Love You Want: A Guide for Couples: Third Edition, Harville Hendrix, PhD and Helen LaKelly Hunt, PhD

It Didn't Start with You: How Inherited Family Trauma Shapes Who We Are and How to End the Cycle, Mark Woylnn

Living and Loving after Betrayal: How to Heal from Emotional Abuse, Deceit, Infidelity, and Chronic Resentment, Steven Stony, PhD

Man's Search for Meaning, Victor E. Frankl

The Myth of Normal: Trauma, Illness and Healing in a Toxic Culture, Dr. Gabor Maté, Daniel Maté

A New Earth: Awakening to Your Life's Purpose, Eckhart Tolle

A Return to Love: Reflections on the Principles of A Course in Miracles, Marianne Williamson

Switch On Your Brain: The Key to Peak Happiness, Thinking, and Health, Dr. Caroline Leaf

The Wisdom of Trauma Documentary, Dr. Gabor Maté

ABOUT THE AUTHOR

Andrea Merkl is a creative consultant, conscious leader, and mother. A forerunner of conscious leadership and purpose-driven marketing, she is blazing new trails in personal transformation and conscious parenting. Having gone through a traumatic experience of infidelity and sexual abuse herself, she has used her own experience to develop a methodology on this subject and is now sharing her unique perspective with audiences and readers, helping others in similar situations. She offers a course on Conscious Co-Parenting, helping families navigate life after divorce and infidelity, providing resources on creating a safe, loving, and collaborative environment for their children.

She resides in Calgary, AB, Canada with her two daughters, co-parenting with their father and step-mom. You will find her running, swimming, biking, and spending time in nature with her family. She believes in the power of transformation, the mind-body connection, and the truth that we are all here to create a better world.

Manufactured by Amazon.ca
Acheson, AB